DESIGNING ARTIFICIAL INTELLIGENCE BASED SOFTWARE

A. Bahrami

Sigma Press- Wilmslow

HALSTED PRESS
a division of JOHN WILEY & SONS. Inc.
605 Third Avenue. New York, N.Y. 10158
New York • Chichester • Brisbane • Toronto • Singapore

First published in 1988 by
Sigma Press 1 South Oak Lane, Wilmslow, SK9 6AR, England.

British Library Cataloguing in Publication Data

Bahrami, Ali
        Designing AI based software.
        1. Computer software - Development
        2. Artificial intelligence
        I. Title
        005.1'2 QA76.76.D47

Library of Congress Cataloguing in Publication Data

Bahrami, Ali.
        Designing AI based software.
        1. Computer software--Development. 2. Artificial
intelligence. 3. Microcomputers--Programming.
I. Title.
QA76.76.D47B34 1988 005.1 87-14729

ISBN (Sigma Press): 1-85058-085-5

ISBN (Halsted Press): 0-470-20912-7

Distributed by
John Wiley & Sons Ltd., Baffins Lane, Chichester, West Sussex, England.

Halsted Press, a division of John Wiely & Sons Inc, 605 Third Avenue, New York, NY 10158, USA

Distributed by
John Wiley & Sons Ltd., Baffins Lane, Chichester, West Sussex, England.

Printed by Interprint Ltd, Malta

Cover design by Professional Graphics, Warrington, UK

PREFACE

Webster's Dictionary defines Intelligence as:

1) The ability to learn or understand or to deal with new or trying situations.

2) The ability to apply knowledge to manipulate one's environment or to think abstractly as measured by objective criteria (as tests) ...

Artificial Intelligence (AI) is a field of science which concerns itself with designing and developing software that is capable of possessing knowledge and applying that knowledge to manipulate an ever changing situation.

"Traditional" and algorithmic processes are unsuitable for problem-solving applications concerned with non-numerical concepts such as ideas, abstract relationships and subjective entities. In order to devise software that can possess intelligence, we must first employ theories and concepts which can deal with these abstract entities. Over the past thirty years or so, many such concepts have been emerged from research in the field of Artificial Intelligence.

Although we do not yet understand human intelligence, we can come close to devising tools which deal with knowledge representation, logic, problem solving metaphors and so on. With the help of these concepts and the aid of symbolic programming languages such as LISP, PROLOG and LOGO, we have the building blocks for designing more powerful software that may possess true intelligence.

The book provides hands-on experimentation for various aspects of machine intelligence and Artificial Intelligence based programs for microcomputers. It first covers the theories of AI, including:

      Knowledge Representation
      Search
      Control and Inference Engines
      Problem Solving
      Logic and Predicate Calculus
      Natural Language Parsing

Next, it employs LISP as the tool to implement these concepts. The book contains a tutorial on LISP programming, which exposes the reader to the basic concepts of LISP language; also included are suggested readings on the subject.

Each chapter contains programming projects to expose the reader to the power of the AI techniques. Some of the projects included in the book are:

An Intelligent Data Base
Vision: A program to recognize different geometric shapes
Expert Systems: A Loan Officer
A Common Sense Reasoning Program
A Generate-and-Test System: A program to solve the travelling salesman problem
A Natural Language Parser.

This book attempts to stimulate the reader and demonstrate the power and sophistication of Artificial Intelligence software by providing a variety of programming projects. It identifies many important concepts and theories that are involved in designing intelligent software, and how these can be implemented in a microcomputer environment.

CONTENTS

Reader Convenience Disk

A disk is available which contains the major program listings contained in this book. The programs are on a 5.25" disk suitable for an IBM PC or compatible; the dialect of LISP used is LISP86, which is based on XLISP, and is readily available.

To obtain the disk, remit £11.50 to Sigma Press; this includes post, packing and VAT and is applicable to the UK and Europe. Overseas purchasers remit £15.00 in pounds sterling (or US $ equivalent) to include airmail despatch.

Sigma Press, 1 South Oak Lane, Wilmslow, Cheshire, SK9 6AR, UK.

1

AN INTRODUCTION TO AI BASED SOFTWARE

Artificial Intelligence, or AI, is the branch of computer science concerned with making computers "intelligent." That goal is still a long way ahead, but over the past thirty years, AI researchers have developed many ideas that have proven practical for a wide variety of applications.

Only a few years ago, the domain of AI software was restricted to mainframe or mini computers and the general public regarded AI software as science fiction. But more powerful microprocessors, such as the Intel 80286/80386 or Motorola 68000/68030 have allowed AI based software to slowly but surely capture the commercial and industrial market. From word-processing to decision support systems, AI based products are being developed for everyone who uses microcomputers.

AI based vs. Traditional Programming

In traditional and algorithmic programming, the program represents knowledge. The programmer has thought out the procedures and steps to solve a problem and the program therefore knows how to solve it. The problem solving is "hard coded" into the program. See Fig 1.1.

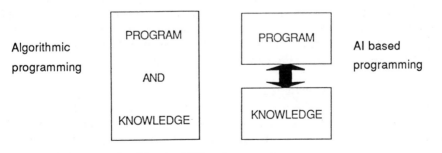

Figure 1.1 Basic Structures of traditional and AI based programming

In contrast, AI based programming does not represent knowledge as part of the program procedures. Instead, it keeps knowledge and program (control) separate and makes the program act as the interpreter. This allows the user to modify or change the knowledge domain and solve different problems without having to change the program itself.

Uniformity of Representation

One of the main ideas behind AI programming and AI programming languages is to represent the program and the data in the same way. Such uniformity of representation allows a program to manipulate programs in the same way that it does data. This ability lets the program learn from the environment by adding to or modifying its functions. Uniformity of representation also allows the program to modify other programs, monitor its own behavior, and explain its reasoning in problem solving.

Modularity

Because it separates knowledge from control, AI based programming tends to be highly modular in design, additions and modifications can be very easy. Therefore the program is not limited by predetermined and predesigned algorithm thought out by the programmer.

Basic Ideas

To understand AI based software, one must understand the basic ideas of symbolic programming, problem and knowledge representation, search, fuzzy sets, symbolic pattern matching, inference-control strategies and problem solving. Chapters 2 to 8 of this book define and explain these ideas fully. Here is a summary of what you will be reading:

Chapter Two: A tutorial on Symbolic Programming Symbolic manipulation programs can recognize particular symbolic expressions. They can take an expression apart to build a new one. Symbol manipulation is a basic building block for AI based software. This book uses the LISP language as an environment for developing software because of it's ability to manipulate symbolic expressions. Some tutorials on LISP are included, with references to more comprehensive reading for interested readers. Chapter 2 may be skipped entirely by LISP programmers.

Chapter Three: Knowledge Representation - The Key to Problem Solving This chapter explores many ideas and theories of knowledge representation and examines some well-defined knowledge representation approaches. These include production systems, frames, slots, links, inheritance, demons, defaults, and semantic networks.

Chapter Four: Search-choosing from Alternatives Search forms the core of AI based software. An AI program, therefore, must use efficient search methods. Chapter four covers search techniques such as breadth-first search, depth-first search, hill-climbing search, best search first, branch and bound search, and A* search.

Chapter Five: Fuzzy Sets Most practical problems are either too complex or too imprecise to be analyzed with a conventional approach. Fuzzy sets break down the complexity and imprecision of a given problem into a managable problem domain without ignoring the important features involved. Fuzzy sets provide a linguistic approach which is the building blocks for dealing with a wide variety of imprecise and complex real-world problems that do not lend themselves to precise analysis in a classical sense such as quantitative techniques of system analysis. This chapter covers the basic idea of linguistic approach to problem solving such as, linguistic variable, linguistic approximation and representation of linguistic hedges.

Chapter Six: Designing Symbolic Pattern Matching Programs A system capable of matching symbolic expressions provides us with a powerful tool, especially for designing and carrying out rule based or expert systems. Chapter six explores this tool and the concept of the "fuzzy matcher."

Chapter Seven: Inference Control Strategies Any type of AI Software is based on the exploitation of some category of abstract reasoning. The general reasoning mechanism has given the AI programs the power to control and manipulate knowledge, in order to reach intelligent conclusions based on available facts. Chapter seven covers some of the well known inference control strategies that have often been used by production rule systems. These are forward-chaining, backward-chaining, mixed strategies, reasoning with reliability factors and fuzzy inference engines.

Chapter Eight: Problem Solving AI based software is all about problem solving. Chapter eight describes another problem-solver paradigm, know as a Generate-and-Test-System. The generate module generates every possible solution and the test module either accepts or rejects it.

AI Based Software for Microcomputers

More and more AI software is available for micros and super micros. The following examples of products provide an insight into what the computer can do, when a program uses AI concepts.

Q & A

Q & A is an integrated word processing and file management software package produced by Symantec Corp. It runs on IBM PC/XT/AT, PS/2 or compatible computers. Q & A contains the "Intelligent Assistant" which is an effective natural language interface. The user can interrogate the data base intuitively and quickly by entering ordinary English phrases and sentences and can ask questions about data and make requests to view forms or to print reports. The Intelligent Assistant contains a vocabulary of 400 words. It learns field names and database contents. The user can train the Assistant to understand new words and so provide more personalized sessions. For example, the user might create a database containing fields that include name, address, city, state, and zip code of concrete suppliers together with prices of the concrete. Once the data base is created we can ask;

```
USER>  WHERE CAN I GET  THE CONCRETE?

Q&A>   SHALL I DO THE FOLLOWING?
       CREATE A REPORT SHOWING THE NAME,
       ADDRESS, CITY, STATE, ZIP AND PRICES FROM ALL
       FORMS?

USER>  SHOW ME THE FORMS FOR THE STATE OF NY.
```

The Q&A will display all the forms for New York.

HAL

HAL, Human Access Language, is a memory resident program from Lotus development Corp. HAL provides a natural interface language for 1-2-3 worksheets. It lets the user make simplified English language requests and refer to the worksheet's columns and rows by their English names or numbers. It can perform English-like commands such as "graph row 1 as bar," to produce a bar chart.

Trigger

Trigger, published by Thoughtware Inc. is a business consultant for managers. It runs on IBM PC/XT/AT, PS/2 or compatible computers. Trigger is based on Thoughtware's "management by exception" concept, which lets the user set up an acceptable limit for his/her organization's performance.

For instance, the manager can assign a normal range of variation to the daily volume of production. If we assume that the normal range of production is from -15% to +20%, then if the production falls below normal by 17% (-17%), certain corrective action is required. Trigger can help the manager to diagnose the cause of the problem and make suggestions for taking corrective actions. Trigger becomes an expert system by learning from past experiences. By tracking causes of problems and corrective actions, it expands its knowledge base. Over time, the more you use it, the better it can get at analysing problems and suggesting solutions.

Expert Choice

Expert Choice, by Decision Support Software Inc. runs on the IBM PC/XT/AT, PS/2 or compatibles. Expert Choice can help decision-makers by forcing them to structure the problems they face. It achieves this by going through lists of preferences, in pairs, making the user decide which is more important. The program helps to identify the most important aspects of a decision, compares alternatives, and provides decisions and the rationale which justifies them. Expert Choice can accommodate both quantitative and subjective judgements. The user can select item X to item Y verbally, rather than numerically, when subjective assignments are more accurate than quantitative one.

The user can express his judgments in three ways: numerically, verbally or graphically. Expert Choice contains what-if features and a rating module for evaluating a large number of alternatives. The user can combine several models and can import information from data bases and spreadsheet.

Expert Choice produces graphic displays of alternative rankings and priorities. It measures the consistency among qualitative judgements and results, to validate decisions.

References

[1].   *"Applications in Artificial Intelligence,"* S. J. Andriole and J. Stephen, Petrocelli Books, Princeton, NJ, 1985.

[2].   *"The Handbook of Artificial Intelligence,"* Barr, Avron, Feigenbaum and A. Edward, Volumes I, II, Wiliam Kaufmann, Los Altos, CA, 1982.

[3].   *"Expert Systems for Microcomputers,"* M. Chadwick and J. Hannah, TAB, Blue Rudge Summit, PA, 1987.

[4].   R. J. Edwards, *"Q & A,"* *Byte*: vol. 11, no. 1, McGraw-Hill, Hancock, NY, 1986.

[5].   *"Artificial Intelligence For Microcomputers The guide for Business Decisionmakers,"* M. Williamson, Brady, New York, NY, 1986.

[6].   *"Artificial Intelligence,"* P.H. Winston, Addison-Wesley, Reading, MA, 1984.

2

A TUTORIAL ON SYMBOLIC PROGRAMMING

Symbol manipulation is the basic building block for AI based software. Symbolic manipulation programs can recognize particular symbolic expressions and can take expressions apart to build new ones.

LISP, or LISt Programming, is a language designed for symbolic manipulation. This book uses LISP-86, a dialect of LISP for microcomputers, for all the programming projects. LISP-86, based on XLISP, developed by David Betz. See note 1.

LISP uses two type of objects, "atoms" and "lists."

Atoms

Atoms are symbols that consist of either numeric or symbolic atoms.

Numeric atoms (also called "numbers") may be positive or negative and may include decimals such as:

2, 2.5, -2.

Symbolic atoms may include words, letters and numbers used as symbols such as:

Lincoln, N25, I, *.

Lists

A list consists of zero or more atoms or lists, enclosed in parenthesis.

Here are five examples of a list.

1. ( )

2. (1)

3. (sigma press)

4. (/ 2 2)

5. (colors (red green blue))

The list 1 is an empty list, which consists of no element, and is written as a set of empty parentheses. The empty list is exactly equivalent to (and will always evaluate to) the symbol NIL. NIL is both a symbol and a list. The list at 2 consists of a numeric atom or number. The list at 3 consists of two members. They are symbolic atoms, "sigma" and "press." The list at 4 consists of the symbol "/" followed by two numeric symbols. The list at 5 consists of two members. The first member is a symbol "colors" and the second member is itself a list "(red green blue)." The point to remember is that lists are enclosed in parentheses. Therefore these are not lists:

```
1

sigma press

/ 2 2
```

The LISP Domain

Because symbolic manipulation is natural to LISP, many programmers have chosen it as a prime developmental tool for intelligent programming. Intelligent programs, written in LISP, exist for areas such as:

Expert systems

Natural language parsing

Common sense reasoning

Learning

Intelligent interface

Vision

Speech

Data base management systems

The list goes on. If we want to learn about intelligent programming, learning about LISP is essential.

LISP has an impact on other areas, such as system programming, symbolic mathematics, and education.

A Tutorial On Basic LISP Ideas

The purpose of this section is to get a flavor of LISP's capability and an introduction to list programming.

The only data structure available to LISP is the list structure. This is not as limiting as it might sound. For example, you can represent a tree structure as a list, as follows:

(root subtree1 subtree2 . . . subtreeN)

The first member of a list is the root. Each subtree is itself a list. The first member of each subtree is a root of that subtree and child of the higher level root. See Fig. 2.1.

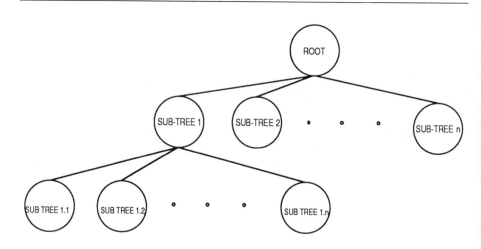

Figure 2.1 A general tree representation of a list.
(ROOT (SUB-TREE.1 SUB-TREE.1.1 SUB-TREE.1.2 ... SUB-TREE.1.n)SUB-TREE.2 ... SUB-TREE.n)

LISP Procedures/Functions

No matter what is in a list, LISP tries to evaluate it by assuming that the first element is the name of a function or procedure and the other elements are the arguments to that function. There are two types of functions in LISP, user-defined functions and system-defined functions. System defined function are also called primitive functions. For example:

```
( + 1 2)
```

The first element of this list is "+" which is a system-defined function. The remaining members of the list (+ 1 2), are arguments for the function "+."

Mathematical Functions

You can add numbers in LISP by simply entering the appropriate function list. For example:

```
>(+ 2 2)

4
```

In the above example the symbol ">" is the LISP interpreter prompt which will appear through out the book.

This simple example provides an insight into LISP's grammar. For LISP to process an expression, the expression must follow these three rules:

RULE 1: An expression is either an atom or a list. If it is a list, it must appear within parentheses.

RULE 2: A space must separate the members of the list. (+ 2 2) is interpreted as 2 + 2, giving the result 4; whereas (+ 22) is interpreted as 22 + 0, giving the result 22.

RULE 3: The first member of a list appears to LISP as a function. The remaining members are the arguments for that function. For example:

```
>  (+ 5 5)
```

The "+" is the function in this list which causes the LISP system to do addition. The two remaining members, 5 and 5, are the arguments for function "+". The expression (+ 5 5) is equivalent to "add 5 to 5." As a general rule in LISP, first state what to do; then state what to do it to.

Matching Parentheses

One of the most important rules in LISP is that the number of opening and closing parentheses must balance. Mismatched parentheses cause the most errors.

Other Mathematical Operations

Other mathematical operations follow the same format as addition. You can subtract, multiply and divide by using the symbols "-", "*" and "/" respectively. For example:

```
> (- 5 4)

1
```

LISP interprets the above expression to (5 - 4) which will result in 1.

```
>(- 2 -1 4 5)

-6
```

The above expression is interpreted to:

```
(2 - (-1) - 4 - 5 ) = -6
```

Note that -1 is an atom which is different from function "-".

```
>(/ 60 10 2)

3
```

In an expression such as above with three or more members, LISP does the operation on the first two members first, then carries the result on to the next member. Therefore it first divide 60 by 10 which result in 6 and then divide the 6 by 2.

FLOAT Function

Numbers may contain decimal places. These number are called floating-point number, and those that do not contain a decimal places are called integer. The FLOAT function is a system function, which converts an integer to a floating point number. For example:

```
>(float 1)

1.00
```

TRUNCATE Function

The TRUNCATE function does the reverse of float. It converts a decimal number to an integer number. For example:

```
> (truncate 1.5)

1
```

Mixing Operations

When a list consists of several sublists, it processes the innermost list first.

```
> (* 10 (- 2 1))
```

The above list consists of three members: "*", 10, and (- 2 1). The innermost list is the list (- 2 1), which LISP processes first and which results in 1. This is followed by:

```
( * 10 1)

10
```

Here are two other examples of mixed operations:

```
>(* (+ -1 5) 2)

8
```

The above expression is evaluated to (* 4 2) which in turn evaluated to 8.

```
>( / (* 2 (- 4 1) ) 2)

3
```

LISP interprets the above expression to: (/ (* 2 3) 2) which is equal to (/ 6 2) and it will evaluate to 3.

Predicate

A predicate is a special function that returns a result which is true or false. In LISP a T represents true and NIL represents false. See Fig 2.2. The following are some of the system-defined predicates:

NUMBERP: This predicate checks to see whether an atom is a number or not.

```
>(numberp 1)

T
```

Here we ask the system whether 1 is a number, The system answers yes. If the atom is non-numeric, the test fails:

```
>(numberp 'john)

NIL
```

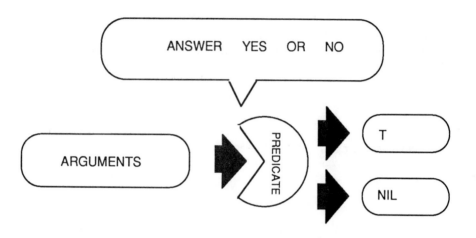

Figure 2.2 A predicate is a procedure that returns either true or false.

SYMBOLP: This predicate checks an atom to see whether it is a symbol. For example:

```
>(symbolp 'john)

T
```

MINUSP: This predicate checks for negative numbers.

```
>(minusp -1)

T
```

Other system-defined predicates include:

```
>(equal 1 1)

T
```

```
>(zerop 1)

NIL

>(oddp 1)

T

>(evenp 2)

T

>(atom 1)

T

>(Listp '(red))

T
```

Function Evaluation

When LISP see a list, it tries to evaluate it by assuming that the first element is the name of a function and the other elements are the arguments for that function. A function's arguments (that can be an atom or a list) must be evaluated before the function can use them. What this means is that the LISP must make sure that all the arguments to a function are appropriate for that function. LISP compares the first element of the list with all the user-defined functions. If it finds a match, it processes the function according to its definition. If it cannot find a match, it tries to find a match with the system-defined functions. If there is no match, the system responds with an error message.

Numbers always evaluate to themselves however, symbols and lists do not with two exceptions. The only symbols that do evaluate to themselves are T and NIL.

```
>5

5

>T

T

>NIL

NIL
```

As we can see from these examples, the LISP respond with the same atom (T, NIL or numbers), because these atoms evaluate to themselves.

The empty list, being equivalent to NIL, is the only list that evaluates to itself.

```
>()

NIL
```

Single Quote

LISP cannot make decisions about evaluating an expression to itself or evaluating by user- defined/system-defined functions. The user must specify where to stop the evaluation by supplying an evaluation stopping signal in the form of the single-quote character. The single quote suspends the LISP function evaluation.

If you type in the list (red green blue) in a LISP environment, without defining a function, such as "red," LISP will respond with an error message. For LISP to evaluate the list (red green blue) to itself, we must type the following:

```
> '(red green blue)

(RED GREEN BLUE)
```

Assignment of Values to Symbolic Atom

Assignment of value to an atom can be done by using a special primitive called SETQ.

SETQ assign the value of its second argument to become the value of the first argument. The argument that we assign a value to, must be a symbol. The following are some example of use of SETQ:

```
>(setq A 2)

2

>A

2

>'A

A
```

In the first example we assign 2 to the symbole A. In the second example LISP has evaluated the symbol A to 2. In the third example symbol A has been evaluated to itself because of the use of the single quote.

Functions Which Manipulate Lists

Many functions take lists as their arguments. Some such as CAR or CDR, return parts of a list; others, such as CONS, LIST, APPEND, build a new one.

LISP has many other built-in functions which operate on lists. These functions provide elegant tools for manipulating symbolic expressions. The pattern which develops in using these functions is:

(Function Argument(1) Argument(2) .. Argument(n))

Argument can be a list or an atom.

The function must not be in quotes.

CAR and CDR

Lists can be visualized as having two parts: the head and the tail. See Fig 2.3. The head of a list is its first element and a tail of a list is the reminder of that list. The primitive functions that can take a list apart are CDR and CAR.

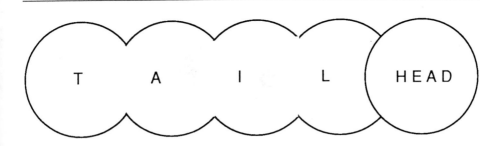

Figure 2.3 A list consists of a head and a tail.

CAR returns the head of a list. See Fig. 2.4. For example:

```
>(car '(a b c))

A

>(car '((a b c) d))

(A B C)
```

15

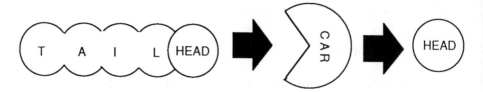

Figure 2.4 CAR will return the head of a list.

In the first example CAR return A because A is the head of the list (A B C). In the second example CAR return the list (A B C) because this is the head of the list ((A B C) D).

CDR returns the tail of a list. See Fig. 2.5. CDR, unlike CAR, always returns a list. For example:

```
>(cdr '(a b c))

(B C)

>(cdr '((a b c) d))

(D)
```

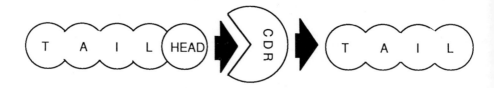

Figure 2.5 CDR will return the tail of a list.

CDR returns the list (B C) in the first example because this list is the tail of the list (A B C). In the second example CDR returns the list (D) because this the tail of the list ((A B C) D).

CAR and CDR can be collapsed into single function. The function that evaluates the CAR of the CDR is called CADR. Likewise, there are functions name CAAR, CDDR and CDAR. LISP-86 only allow up to two level of combination of CAR and CDR. Let's look at the following examples:

```
>(car (cdr '(a b c)))

B
```

The reason for this is that LISP always starts the evaluation at the deepest level of embedding parenthesis and move outward. Therefore LISP first tries to evaluate '(A B C) which will evaluate to itself. Next it tries to evaluate (CDR '(A B C)) which evaluates to (B C), next it applies the CAR to the list (B C) which is B. The short cut to do this would be to use CADR as follows:

```
>(cadr '(a b c))

B
```

Now let's look at CDDR:

```
>(cdr (cdr '(a b c))

(C)
```

Again LISP evaluates from deepest level outword. New let's use the shortcut as follows:

```
(CDDR '(a b c))

(C)
```

Do some experimentation with CAAR and CDAR, these are equivalent to CAR of CAR and CDR of CAR respectively.

Building an Expression

CONS

CONS is an important function, which can construct a list from its arguments. CONS adds an element to the beginning of a list. That element becomes the head of the new list. See Fig 2.6. For example:

```
>(cons 'first '(second third))

(FIRST SECOND THIRD)

>(cons '(ONE) '(TWO THREE))

((ONE) TWO THREE)
```

```lisp
            (press_a_key) ;Wait.
            (gc)                ;Perform garbage
                                ;collections.
            (initialize)
            (display))      ;Clear the window.
        )
    )
)
;     draw
; Perform the line drawing.

(defun draw (command)
    (let (
        (x   (nth 1 command))
        (y   (nth 2 command)))
        (cond
            ((member 'disconnect command)  ;Display
                                           ;the cursor.
                (move (+ x 100) (+ y 50))
                (point (+ x 100) (+ y 50))
                (setq oldx  x  oldy  y ));Save the
                                        ;new location.
            ((member 'draw command)        ;Draw the
                                           ;line.
                (line-rel  (- x oldx) (- y oldy) )
                (setq oldx x  oldy  y ))
        )
    )
)
;     initialize

(defun initialize ()
        (setq scene '() coor '() group '() oldx 0
                                          oldy 0
            h_list '() v_list '() d_list '())
)
;       add_list
; Add new item to Associate list.
(defun add_list (lst item )
        (append lst (list item))
)
;       closep
; This predicate check to see whether or not
; the shape is closed.

(defun closep (lst)
```

```lisp
        (if (equal (co_ords_of_input 0 lst)   ;Closed
                   (co_ords_of_input 0 (last lst)))
                T
                NIL
        )
)
;      recognize
; The procedure recognize the scene by classifying
; the shape according to production rules.

(defun recognize ()
    (do*
        ((i 0 (+ i 1))     ;Do the cycle of matching &
                           ;firing.
        (lst (nth i scene) (nth i scene)))
        ((= i (length scene)))
        (setq h_list '() v_list '() d_list '())
                           ;Reset the lists.
        (rule1 lst)        ;Put horizontal lines into
                           ;h_list.
        (rule2 lst)        ;Put vertical lines into
                           ;v_list.
        (rule3 lst)        ;Put diagonal lines into
                           ;d_list.
            (cond
                ((not (closep lst))  ;Is not closed ?
                    (display_result i h_list v_list
                                    d_list))
                ((= (- (length lst) 1) 3)  ;Triangle?
                    (rule4 i lst))
                ((= (- (length lst) 1) 4)  ;Rectangle?
                    (rule5 i lst h_list v_list))
        )
    )
)
;      rule1
; RULE #1: IF y(a)= y(b) THEN the line (ab) is
; horizontal.

(defun rule1 (ls)
    (do*
        ((i 0 (+ i 1))
        (f (co_ords_of_input i ls)
           (co_ords_of_input i ls))
        (n (co_ords_of_input (+ i 1) ls)
           (co_ords_of_input (+ i 1) ls)))
```

```lisp
                        ((= i (- (length ls) 1)))
                            (if (equal (cdr f)(cdr n));Horizontal?
                                (setq h_list              ;Add it to the
                                                          ;Horizontal list
                                    (append h_list (list (nth i ls))
                                    (list (nth (+ i 1) ls))))
                                )
                    )
)
;              rule2
; RULE #2: IF x(a)= x(b) THEN the line (ab) is
; vertical.

(defun rule2 (ls)
    (do*
        ((i 0 (+ i 1))
        (f (co_ords_of_input i ls)
            (co_ords_of_input i ls))
        (n (co_ords_of_input (+ i 1) ls)
            (co_ords_of_input (+ i 1) ls)))
        ((= i (- (length ls) 1)))
            (if (equal (car f)(car n))  ;Vertical?
                (setq v_list              ;added it to
                                          ;the Vertical
                                          ;list.
                    (append v_list (list (nth i ls))
                    (list (nth (+ i 1) ls))))
                )
        )
)
;      rule3
; RULE #2: IF x(a) /= x(b) AND y(a) /= y(b)
;          THEN the line (ab) is diagonal.

(defun rule3 (ls)
    (do*
        ((i 0 (+ i 1))
        (f (co_ords_of_input i ls)
            (co_ords_of_input i ls))
        (n (co_ords_of_input (+ i 1) ls)
            (co_ords_of_input (+ i 1) ls)))
        ((= i (- (length ls) 1)))
            (if (and (not(equal (car f)(car n)))
                              ;Diagonal?
            (not (equal (cdr f)(cdr n))))
```

```lisp
                    (setq d_list   ;Add it to Diagonal
                                   ;list.
                      (append d_list (list   (nth i ls))
                      (list (nth (+ i 1) ls))))
       )
    )
)
;      rule4
; RULE #4:  IF it is closed AND has three sides
;           THEN the shape is Triangle.

(defun rule4 (n lst)
        (display_result n '() '() '() 'Triangle)
)
;      rule5
; RULE #5: IF it is closed
;            AND 2 of its sides are horizontal
;            AND other 2 sides are vertical
;            Then the shape is Rectangle.

(defun rule5 (n lst h_list v_list)
    (if (and (= (/ (length h_list) 2) 2)
        (= (/ (length v_list) 2) 2))
                   (display_result n '() '() '()
                                   'Rectangle)
    )
)


;      display_result
;
(defun display_result (n h_list v_list d_list
                                 &optional shape)
    (move-cursor n 0)
    (cond
      ((not (null shape))
         (print `(shape ,n is a ,shape)))
      ((not (null h_list))
         (print_line h_list 'Horizental))
      ((not (null v_list))
         (print_line v_list 'Vertical))
      ((not (null d_list))
         (print_line d_list 'Diagonal))
    )
)


;      print_line
```

60

```lisp
; Report the type of line.

(defun print_line (lst type)
        (do*
            ((i 0 (+ i 2))
             (f (co_ords_of_input i lst)
                (co_ords_of_input i lst))
             (n (co_ords_of_input (+ i 1) lst)
                (co_ords_of_input (+ i 1) lst)))
            ((> i (- (length lst) 1)))
            (print `(,type line from ,f to ,n))
        )
)
;       display
; Display the window.

(defun display ()
        (init 4)                ;Graphics mode LISP-86
                                ;primitive.
        (rectangle 99 49 249 149 2);Draw rectangle
                                ;LISP-86 primitive.
        (move-cursor 5 11)(print '(0 0)) ;Move
                                ;cursor LISP-86 primitive
        (move-cursor 5 28)(print '(150 0))
        (move-cursor 19 9)(print '(0 100))
        (move-cursor 19 28)(print '(150 100))
)
;       get_input.
; Get input strings.

(defun get_input ()
        (clear_line 23 0)
        (move-cursor 23 0)
        (princ "COMMAND LINE:")
        (read)
)
;       press_a_key
; Wait until user presses a key.

(defun press_a_key ()
        (clear_line 23 0)
        (move-cursor 23 10)
        (princ "Press C to continue ")
        (read)
)
;       clear_line
```

```
; Clear the command line.

(defun clear_line (r c)
        (move-cursor r c)
        (do (( i 0 (+ i 1)))
                ((= i (- 40 c)))
                (princ " ")
        )
)


;           co_ords_of_input
; Get the co-ordinate
(defun co_ords_of_input (n ls)
                (cdr (assoc (nth n ls) coor))
        )
```

The Function VISION starts the program by first initializing all the global lists. These global lists include:

1. SCENE is a list of lists. Each sublist is an entity of the scene. These entities contain vertices which describe a closed or an open plane. For instance, SCENE may contain:

   SCENE = ((0 1 2 3) (5 6))

See Fig. 3.4. As we can see, this list describes two entities, a triangle and a horizontal line.

2. COOR is an associative list which contains the vertices along with their co-ordinates. The COOR for Fig. 3.4 is:

   COOR = ((0 10 10) (1 100 10) (2 50 50) (3 10 10) (4 90 90) (5 10 90))

3. At each phase of constructing the scene, a global variable GROUP contains a group of the points which together yield an entity in the scene.

4. The lists H_LIST, V_LIST, and D_LIST, at each step in the analysis phase, contain the list of horizontal, vertical, and diagonal lines, respectively.

The procedure DISPLAY will draw the input window, see Fig. 3.5.

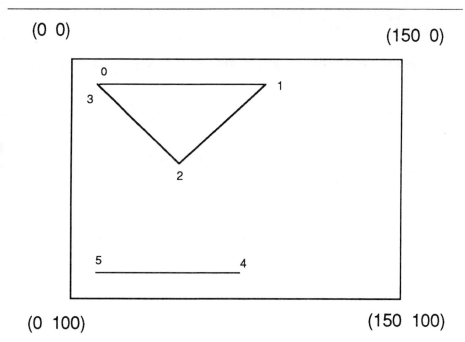

(0 0)　　　　　　　　　　　　　　　(150 0)

(0 100)　　　　　　　　　　　　　　(150 100)

Figure 3.5 Two entities in this scene are lists (0 1 2 3) and (4 5).

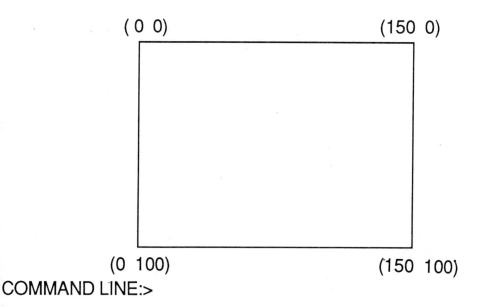

(0 0)　　　　　　　　　　　　　　(150 0)

(0 100)　　　　　　　　　　　　　　(150 100)

COMMAND LINE:>

Figure 3.6

The procedure PROCESS_COMMAND reads the input strings and calls the appropriate procedures to perform the command.

In order to understand how this program works, let's go through creating a scene and see what will happen at each step.

STEP 1. The user must tell the system to move the cursor to an appropriate location. The keyword to use is "disconnect."

For example, if we want to move the cursor to co-ordinate (10 10) on the input window, type: (disconnect 10 10)

Another purpose of "disconnect" is that it tells the system we are working on a new entity of the scene. See Fig 3.7.

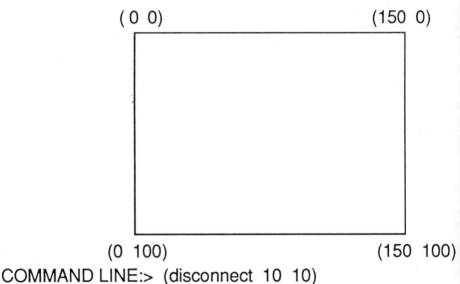

(0 0)   (150 0)

(0 100)   (150 100)
COMMAND LINE:> (disconnect 10 10)

Figure 3.7

STEP 2. Once the system has been told the beginning point, we can start to draw our triangle by typing:

(draw 100 10)

This command causes the system to draw from the previous point (10 10) to the new (x, y) co-ordinate (100 10). (See Fig. 3.8, 3.8, 3.10, 3.4.)

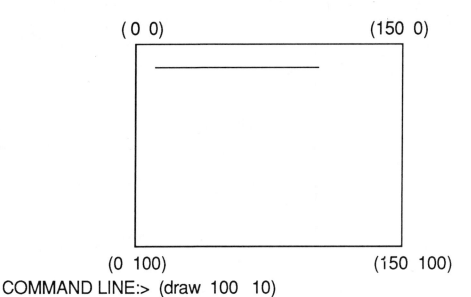

COMMAND LINE:> (draw 100 10)

Figure 3.8

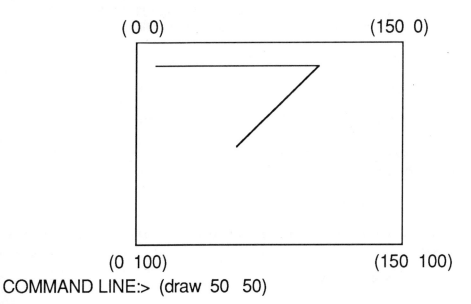

COMMAND LINE:> (draw 50 50)

Figure 3.9

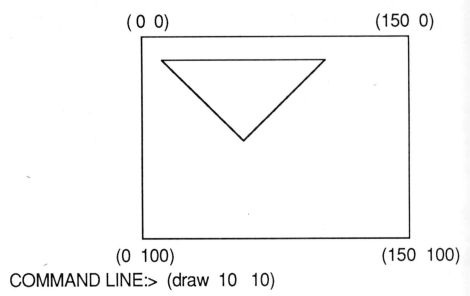

COMMAND LINE:> (draw 10   10)

Figure 3.10

While we are busy drawing our triangle, the procedure PROCESS_COMMAND is busy updating the global lists SCENE, GROUP, and COOR. Now these lists contain:

SCENE = ()

GROUP = (0 1 2 3)

COOR = ((0 10 10) (1 100 10) (2 50 50) (3 10 10))

At this point, if we want to draw a new horizontal line from (90 90) to (10 90), we must first type:

(disconnect 90 90)

This command will move the cursor to the point (90 90) and update our global list as follows:

SCENE = ((0 1 2 3))

GROUP = (4)

COOR = ((0 10 10) (1 100 10) (2 50 50) (3 10 10) (4 90 90))

```
;              Graph3.dat
; This data base represents the graph in Figure 4.7
;


(R)

(R Parent (P Q))
(P Parent (A B))
(Q Parent (E F))
(A Parent (C D))
(F Parent (G H))

(R X (10))
(R Y (22))

(P X (10))
(P Y (5))

(Q X (5))
(Q Y (15))

(A X (20))
(A Y (10))

(B X (5))
(B Y (10))

(C X (30))
(C Y (15))

(D X (12))
(D Y (25))

(E X (7))
(E Y (8))

(F X (30))
(F Y (45))

(G X (50))
(G Y (10))

(H X (10))
(H Y (10))
```

Let's ask our hill climbing procedure to search for the node H.

```
(PLEASE ENTER THE NODE TO BE SEARCH FOR ?)> H

(VISITING NODE R)
(VISITING NODE Q)
(VISITING NODE E)
(VISITING NODE F)
(VISITING NODE H)
(TARGET H IS FOUND)
```

Hill climbing search has selected nodes Q in place of P, and E instead of F, because Q and E are closer than P and F, respectively (compare this with the outcome of depth first search).

Following is the program listing for hill climbing search.

```
(defun HILL_CLIMBING ()
      (setq graph                ;Open data base.
         (open_file "graph.dat" ':INPUT ))
      (read_data graph)          ;Read the graph.
      (close graph)
      (report (hc                ;Perform hill climbing.
            ROOT (ask_node) ROOT))
)
;
;      open_file
; This function simply opens the file to read or
; write.

(defun open_file (fname read-write)
      (open fname :direction read-write)
)
;
;      read_data
; This function reads data from the data base.
;
   (defun read_data (graph)
      (setq root (read graph)) ;Get the root.
      (do ()
            ((null (property_list (read graph ))))

      )
)
;       property_list
; Set up a property list to represent a graph.
```

```
(defun property_list (item)
    (cond
        ((null item) nil)
        (T                              ;Assign children to
                                        ;parent.
            (property item))
    )
)
;
;       property
; Assign property name and property symbol to a
; symbol

(defun property (item)
        (setf (get (car item) (cadr item))
              (car (cddr item))))
)
;
;       hc
;
(defun hc (tour target visited)
    (visiting (car tour))
    (cond
        ((null tour) nil)           ;Boundary condition.
        ((equal (car tour) target) target) ;Target is
                                           ;found.
        (T
          (hc
                (append (visit tour     ;Replace it with
                                        ;the children.
                            (sort '()   ;Sort the
                                        ;children first.
                                (children (car tour))
                                        target)
                                visited) (cdr tour))
                target (append visited (list(car tour))))))
        )
    )
)
;       visit
; Check to see if children are in the tour. If so
; do not include them again. Otherwise  add those
; ones that are not in the tour.

(defun visit (tour children visited)
    (cond
```

107

```lisp
        ((null children) '())
        ((or(member (car children) visited)
            (member (car children) tour))
            (visit tour (cdr children) visited))
        (T
            (append (list (car children))
                (visit tour (cdr children)
                                    visited)))
        )
)


;
(defun children (node )
    (get node 'parent)            ;Get the children.
)
;
;      sort
; Perform insertion sort.
(defun sort (lst1 lst2 target)
    (cond
        ((null lst2) lst1) ;Boundry condition.
        (T                ;Otherwise sort the rest.
            (sort (insert lst1 (car lst2) target)
                    (cdr lst2) target))
    )
)
;
;      insert
; Insert a node in a sorted list.
(defun insert (lst item target)
    (cond
        ((null item ) lst)              ;Return the list.
        ((null lst ) (list item))       ;Boundary.
        ((<(distance item target)       ;Sort it.
            (distance (car lst) target))
                (append (list item) lst))
        (T                      ;Go deeper.
                (append (list (car lst))
                        (insert (cdr lst) item
                                    target)))
    )
)
;
;      distance
; Calculate a distance between two nodes by using
; straight
```

```lisp
; line distance.

(defun distance (node1 node2)
(let (( x1 (car (get node1 'x)))
      ( x2 (car (get node2 'x)))
      ( y1 (car (get node1 'y)))
      ( y2 (car (get node2 'y))))
      (+
           (* (- x1 x2) (- x1 x2))
           (* (- y1 y2) (- y1 y2)))
   )
)
;
(defun report (target)
      (if (null target)
           (print '(Sorry cannot find the target))
           (print `(Target ,target is found))
      )
      (terpri)
)
;
(defun visiting (node)
      (print `(Visiting node ,node))
)
;
;      ask_node
(defun ask_node ()
      (terpri)
      (print `(Please enter the node to be searched
                                    for ? ))
      (read)
)
```

We have added three new procedures to our depth first search. These are SORT, INSERT, and DISTANCE.

The procedure SORT orders a list according to estimate of remaining distance. We are using a sorting technique called an insertion sort. SORT takes three arguments. These are:

LST1: Sorted list.

LST2: A list to be sorted.

TARGET: The goal state to be used for ordering.

The procedure SORT uses INSERT to insert a node in the sort list. The procedure INSERT places a node in the sorted node, depending on the distance to the target node.

The only major difference between the procedure hill climbing and DFS is that hill climbing first sorts the children of a node according to their straight-line distance to the target node, before visiting them.

Best First Search

Best first search is a hill climbing search with only one difference. Unlike hill climbing, which sorts children of a node under consideration and selects the most promising among them to search, best first search progresses in the best direction by sorting all the nodes in the list TOUR and then selecting the most promising among them to search. Here is the algorithm for best first search:

I   Repeat until all the nodes in the search space have been examined.

    I.1 Check the head of the list of nodes under consideration. If it is the goal state report back the success and stop; otherwise continue.

    I.2 Replace the node at head of the list with its children (if it has any). I.3 Sort (by remaining cost) the entire list.

    I.3 Sort the entire list.

Using the graph in Fig 4.7, let's see how best first search will explore the nodes.

```
(PLEASE ENTER THE NODE TO BE SEARCHED FOR ?)> D

(VISITING NODE R)

(VISITING NODE Q)

(VISITING NODE E)

(VISITING NODE P)

(VISITING NODE B)

(VISITING NODE A)

(VISITING NODE D)

(TARGET D IS FOUND)
```

We can achieve best first search by changing the hill climbing algorithm so that it sorts all the nodes in TOUR, instead of only children of the node under consideration.

Following is the program listing for best first search.

```
;
;      bstfs
;
(defun bstfs (tour target visited)
    (visiting (car tour))
    (cond
       ((null tour) nil)         ;Boundary condition.
       ((equal (car tour) target) target) ;Target is
                                           ;found.
       (T
         (bstfs
            (sort '()            ;Sort the whole tour.
               (append (visit tour    ;Replace it with
                                       ;its children.
                  (children (car tour)) visited)
                  (cdr tour))
               target)
            target (append visited (list(car tour))))
       )
    )
)
```

Best first search combines the advantages of depth first search and breadth first search strategies, Since the search proceeds along a tree, but unlike DFS the selection at each branch point is not arbitrary, but is based on best direction from the best node examined so far.

Finding The Shortest Path

So far we have studied four searching strategies that can find the goal state without considering what is the shortest or the least-cost path to the goal state.

This section discusses two searching algorithms that provide us with the shortest path to the goal state.

Branch And Bound Search

One way to find the least-cost path to the goal state is to first generate all the possible paths, using depth first search or breadth first search. Then we select the least-cost path among the generated paths that lead to the goal state. This technique is known as the British Museum Algorithm and no one would seriously consider using it, because it would take longer than most of us can imagine to accomplish anything.

A better way is a technique called branch and bound search.

Assume we would like to find the least-cost path to the node E. (See Fig 4.8.) Further assume that certain costs are involved in traversing from one node to another.

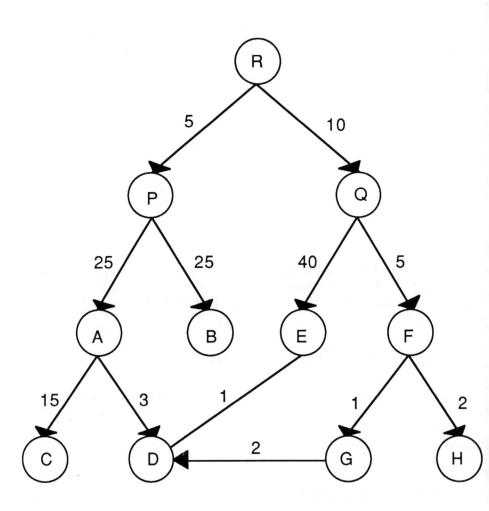

Figure 4.8 The numbers beside the links are cost of visiting the node from its parent.

Branch and bound will find the least-cost path to the goal state by employing the following algorithm:

I   Repeat until all the nodes in the search space have been examined.

    I.1   Check the head of the list of paths, to see if it leads to the goal state. If it does, report the success and stop, otherwise continue.

    I.2   Extend the node at the head of the list of paths by one level. This will result in creating many new paths.

    I.3   Sort all the paths in the list by their accumulated cost so that the least-cost path will be at the head of the list.

Since the procedure selects the least-cost path for extension, the path that first reaches the goal state is guaranteed to be the least-cost path.

As usual, we have to first revise our data base to accommodate new changes. The new property name for the cost of traversing from one node to another node must be created. Following is the new data base to represent the graph in Fig. 4.8.

```
;                   Graph4.dat
; This data base represents the graph in Figure 4.8.
;

(R 0)                        ;Graph name.

(R Parent ((P 5) (Q 10)))

(P Parent ((A 20) (B 25)))

(Q Parent ((E 40) (F 5)))

(A Parent ((C 15) (D 3)))

(F Parent ((G 1) (H 2)))

(G Parent ((D 2)))

(D Parent ((E 1)))
```

The following demonstrates how branch and bound selects the least-cost path for an extension that eventually results in finding the least-cost path.

```
(PLEASE ENTER THE NODE TO BE SEARCHED FOR ?)> E

(PATHS> ((R 0)))
(PATHS> ((R P 5) (R Q 10)))
(PATHS> ((R Q 10) (R P A 25) (R P B 30)))
```

```
(PATHS> ((R Q F 15) (R P A 25) (R P B 30) (R Q E
          50)))
(PATHS> ((R Q F G 16) (R Q F H 17) (R P A 25) (R P B
          30)
          (R Q E 50)))
(PATHS> ((R Q F H 17) (R Q F G D 18) (R P A 25) (R P
          B 30)
          (R Q E 50)))
(PATHS> ((R Q F G D 18) (R P A 25) (R P B 30) (R Q E
          50)))
(PATHS> ((R Q F G D E 19) (R P A 25) (R P B 30) (R Q
          E 50)))

The least-cost path to the target is:(R Q F G D E)
(TOTAL COST (19))
```

The number that is tagged along each path represents the accumulated cost of traversing. As we see, the least-cost path always expands first. At a third try, the procedure finds a path (R Q E 50) which leads to the goal state E. But since the path (R Q F 15) is cheaper to expand than other paths, branch and bound keeps exploring that path which finally leads to the least-cost path (R Q F G D E).

See the program listing, as follows:

```
(defun BEST_PATH ()
      (setq graph                ;Open data base.
          (open_file "graph.dat" ':INPUT ))
      (read_data graph)          ;Read the graph.
      (close graph)
      (report (bab               ;Perform Branch and
                                 ;bound.
          (list ROOT ) (ask_node)))
)
;
;      open_file
; This function simply opens the file to read or
; write

(defun open_file (fname read-write)
      (open fname :direction read-write)
)
;
;      read_data
; This function reads data from the data base.
;
(defun read_data (graph)
```

114

```lisp
          (setq root (read graph)) ;Get the root.
          (do ()
               ((null (property_list (read graph )))))

          )
)
;        property_list
; Set up a property list to represent a graph.
;
(defun property_list (item)
     (cond
        ((null item) nil)
        (T                              ;Assign children to
                                        ;parent.
             (property item))
     )
)
;
;        property
; Assign property name and property symbol to a
; symbol

(defun property (item)
        (setf (get (car item) (cadr item))
              (car (cddr item)))
)
;
;        bab
;
(defun bab (tour target )
     (print`(PATHS> ,tour))
     (cond
        ((null tour) nil)           ;Boundary condition.
        ((goalp (car tour) target)
                     (car tour)) ;Target is found.
        (T                          ;Otherwise.
        (bab
          (sort '()                 ;Sort the whole tour.
               (append (path (car tour) target)
                     (cdr tour)))
        target))
     )
)
;        goalp
(defun goalp (tour target)
     (let ((tail                     ;Lead to a target?
```

```lisp
                 (cadr (reverse tour)))))
       (cond
             ((equal tail target) T)  ;Yes.
             (T nil)                  ;No.
       )
    )
)
;
;     path
;
(defun path (p target)
    (let (( c                      ;Get children.
                (children (cadr (reverse p))))
            (cost (car (last p)))      ;Cost so far.
            (p1 (reverse (cdr (reverse p))))))
            (cond
                ((goalp p target) p)     ;Do not expand
                                         ;it.
                ((null c) '())
                (T (path1 p1 c cost))    ;Expand the
                                         ;path.
            )
    )
)
;
;     path1
;
(defun path1 (p c cost)
    (cond
       ((null c) '())              ;Boundary condition.
       (T                          ;Create paths.
           (cons
             (append p             ;Expand the path.
                    (list (caar c)
                         (cost (car c) cost)))
                    (path1 p (cdr c) cost)))
    )
)
;     cost
(defun cost (c t)
       (+ (car (last c)) t)      ;Add cost of children.
)
;
;     children
;
(defun children (node )
```

116

```lisp
        (get node 'parent) ;Get the children.
)
;            sort
; Perform insertion sort.
(defun sort (tour paths)
    (cond
        ((null paths) tour)    ;Boundry condition.
        (T                     ;Sort the rest.
            (sort (insert tour (car paths))
                (cdr paths)))
    )
)
;
;            insert
; Insert a node in a sorted list.
(defun insert (tour p)
    (cond
        ((and (null p)(null tour)) '()) ;Nil.
        ((null p) tour)          ;Return the list.
        ((null tour) (list p)) ;Boundary condition.
        ((cheap p (car tour))
                (cons p tour));Put it at the head.
        (T                       ;Otherwise go deeper.
            (cons (car tour)
                (insert (cdr tour) p)))
    )
)
;      cheap
; This predicate finds out which path has the least
; accumulated cost and least amount of remaining
; cost.
(defun cheap (p1 p2)
    (if
        (<=                     ;Cheapest so far.
            (car (last p1))
            (car (last p2)))
                T     ;Yes.
                Nil   ;No.
    )
)
;      report
;
(defun report (tour)
    (let ((p (reverse (cdr (reverse tour))))
            (cost (last tour)))
        (cond
```

```
                    ((null tour)        ;Report the failure.
                        (princ "\nSorry cannot find the
                                            target"))
                    (T                   ;Report the success.
                        (princ "\nThe least-cost path to
                                    the target is:")
                        (print p)    ;Display the least-cost
                                     ;path.
                        (print `(Total cost ,cost)))
            )
        (terpri)
      )
  )
  ;
  ;       ask_node
  (defun ask_node ()
        (terpri)
        (print `(Please enter the node to be searched
                                        for ?))
        (read)

  )
```

The program BEST_PATH is very like our last program, best first search, with the following modifications.

The list TOUR is a list of lists and each sub- list represents an incomplete path. Another addition is the predicate GOALP, which examines a path to see if it leads to the goal state.

Predicate GOALP takes two arguments. These are a list which represents a path, and the goal state node. Goal returns T or Nil, depending on whether the last node in the path list is the goal node.

The procedure PATH expands a path at the head of the list TOUR. PATH takes two arguments: the path to be expanded and the target node. If the path under consideration has already reached the goal state or a terminal node, PATH will not expand it any further. Otherwise it gets the list of children of the last node in the path under consideration. It will then call procedure PATH1 to create as many incomplete paths as there are children.

Procedure PATH1 takes three arguments. These are:

P: The path needed to be expanded.

C: The list of children of the last node in the list P.

COST: The accumulated cost so far.

This recursive procedure appends the child node, along with the accumulate cost, to the path. In other words, it extends the path by one level.

For example, PATH takes the list (R Q 10) and returns (R Q E 40) and (R Q F 15), as long as Q is not the target node.

Procedure COST takes two arguments, the cost of traversing to the child node and the accumulated cost. It adds these costs and returns the new accumulated cost.

We can improve the efficiency of branch and bound by eliminating all the paths that lead to the same node except the one with the minimum cost. This example makes this point clear:

```
(PLEASE ENTER THE NODE TO BE SEARCHED FOR ?)> A
(PATHS> ((R 0)))
(PATHS> ((R P 5) (R Q 10)))
(PATHS> ((R Q 10) (R P A 25) (R P B 30)))
(PATHS> ((R Q F 15) (R P A 25) (R P B 30) (R Q E
                                                50)))
(PATHS> ((R Q F G 16) (R Q F H 17) (R P A 25) (R P B
                             30) (R Q E 50)))
(PATHS> ((R Q F H 17) (R Q F G D 18) (R P A 25) (R P
                       B 30) (R Q E 50)))
(PATHS> ((R Q F G D 18) (R P A 25) (R P B 30) (R Q E
                                                50)))
(PATHS> ((R Q F G D E 19) (R P A 25) (R P B 30) (R Q
                                          E 50)))
(PATHS> ((R P A 25) (R P B 30) (R Q E 50)))

The least-cost path to the target is:(R P A)
(TOTAL COST (25))
```

Although a path (R Q F G D E 19) is found that leads to node E, the path (R Q E 50) has remained in the list to be expanded. Since there is a cheaper path to the node E, there is no need to consider the path (R Q E). We can eliminate this path and forget it forever.

The following is the revised version of procedure BAB.

```
;
;      bab
;
(defun bab (tour target )
    (print` (PATHS: ,tour))
    (cond
        ((null tour) nil)         ;Boundary condition.
```

119

```
            ((goalp (car tour) target)
                    (car tour))  ;Target is found.
      (T                         ;Otherwise.
         (bab
           (sort '()             ;Sort the whole tour.
             (common (path (car tour) target)
                 (cdr tour)))
           target))
      )
)


;      common
; If two or more paths reach a common node, delete
; all those paths except the path that reaches the
; node with the least cost.

(defun common (p l)
     (let ((hp (car p))
           (tp (cdr p))
           (hl (car l))
           (tl (cdr l)))
       (cond
          ((and (null p) (not (null l)))
                       l)
          ((and (null l) (not (null p)))
                       p)
          ((and (null l) (null p))
                       '())
          ((equal (cadr (reverse hp))
                  (cadr (reverse hl)))
                       (cons (car
                             (insert (list hp) hl))
                       (common tp tl)))
          (T                     ;Compare it with the
                                 ;rest.
                       (cons hl (common p tl)))
          )
        )
     )
```

We have replaced APPEND with the procedure COMMON. COMMON takes two
arguments. These are;

P: The new extended paths,

L: The list of the paths.

COMMON appends the new extended paths to the list of the paths and eliminates all the paths that reach a common node except the one with the minimum cost.

Now lest see how the new version of branch and bond will behave.

```
(PLEASE ENTER THE NODE TO BE SEARCHED FOR ?)> B

(PATHS> ((R 0)))
(PATHS> ((R P 5) (R Q 10)))
(PATHS> ((R Q 10) (R P A 25) (R P B 30)))
(PATHS> ((R Q F 15) (R P A 25) (R P B 30) (R Q E
                                               50)))
(PATHS> ((R Q F G 16) (R Q F H 17) (R P A 25) (R P B
                               30) (R Q E 50)))
(PATHS> ((R Q F H 17) (R Q F G D 18) (R P A 25) (R P
                          B 30) (R Q E 50)))
(PATHS> ((R Q F G D 18) (R P A 25) (R P B 30) (R Q E
                                               50)))
(PATHS> ((R Q F G D E 19) (R P A 25) (R P B 30)))
(PATHS> ((R P A 25) (R P B 30)))
(PATHS> ((R P A D 28) (R P B 30) (R P A C 40)))
(PATHS> ((R P A D E 29) (R P B 30) (R P A C 40)))
(PATHS> ((R P B 30) (R P A C 40)))

The least-cost path to the target is:(R P B)
(TOTAL COST (30))
```

Notice that, once a path (R Q F G D E) has been found, the other path to E, namely (R Q E), is eliminated from the list TOUR. This will improve the system's overall efficiency by reducing the number of paths it considers.

A* Search

A* search is a branch and bound search with one additional feature, the knowledge of the remaining cost for each path under consideration. This addition allows A* search to produce optimal solutions.

A* will find the least-cost path to the goal state by employing the following algorithm:

I   Repeat until all the nodes in the search space have been examined.

    I.1 Check the head of the list of paths, to see if it leads to the goal state. If it does, report the success and stop, otherwise continue.

    I.2 Extend the node at the head of the list of paths by one level. This will result in creating many new paths.

    I.3 Sort all the paths in the list by the estimate of their remaining cost so that the most promising path will be at the head of the list.

Although we may not know the actual cost of the remaining cost in advance, we can substitute an estimate for the actual cost.

In our heuristic approach for implementing the A* search, we will use the least-cost path that one can take from a given node to a leaf (terminal node). The motivation behind using this estimate is that if the least-cost path to a leaf contains the goal node, this path is also the least-cost path to the goal node. For instance, in Fig. 4.8 let's assume that out goal node is node D, two paths lead to the goal node D these are:

     Path1: (R P A D)
     Path2: (R Q F G D)

The cost of getting to the leaf from path1 is 29 (adding 5, 20, 3 and 1) and for path2 is 19 (adding 10, 5, 1, 2, 1). Path2 also contains the least-cost path to the goal node D (the cost to the goal node D for path2 is 18 vs. 28 for path1). Let's revise our data base to reflect this new addition.

```
;                    Graph5.dat
; This data base represents the graph in Fig. 4.8.
; With new addition of property name and value of
; estimate cost form given node to a leaf.

(R 0)                      ;Graph name.

(R Parent ((P 5) (Q 10)))

(P Parent ((A 20) (B 25)))

(Q Parent ((E 40) (F 5)))

(A Parent ((C 15) (D 3)))

(F Parent ((G 1) (H 2)))

(G Parent ((D 2)))

(D Parent ((E 1)))


(R Estimate (17))

(P Estimate (24))

(A Estimate (4))

(D Estimate (1))
```

```
(Q Estimate (7))

(F Estimate (2))

(G Estimate (3))

(C Estimate (0))

(E Estimate (0))

(H Estimate (0))

(B Estimate (0))
```

As we can see from our data base, each node has a property name ESTIMATE which is its distance from the leaf.

Asking the same question from our A* search, we will have:

```
(PLEASE ENTER THE NODE TO BE SEARCHED FOR ?)> B

(PATHS> ((R 0)))
(PATHS> ((R P 5) (R Q 10)))
(PATHS> ((R Q 10) (R P A 25) (R P B 30)))
(PATHS> ((R Q F 15) (R P A 25) (R P B 30) (R Q E
                                                50)))
(PATHS> ((R Q F G 16) (R Q F H 17) (R P A 25) (R P B
                                30) (R Q E 50)))
(PATHS> ((R Q F H 17) (R Q F G D 18) (R P A 25) (R P
                         B 30) (R Q E 50)))
(PATHS> ((R Q F G D 18) (R P A 25) (R P B 30) (R Q E
                                                50)))
(PATHS> ((R Q F G D E 19) (R P A 25) (R P B 30)))
(PATHS> ((R P A 25) (R P B 30)))
(PATHS> ((R P B 30) (R P A C 40) (R P A D 28)))

The least-cost path to the target is:(R P B)
(TOTAL COST (30))
```

In contrast to branch and bound search, the A* search has selected the path (R P B) to (R P A) because of its lower remaining cost.

```
(defun BEST_PATH ()
      (setq graph                  ;Open data base.
            (open_file "graph.dat" ':INPUT ))
```

Consider now modeling the phrase "very low." How should we design the hedge "very," so that it yields a fuzzy set that qualifies intuitively for the phrase "very low" ? Assume that we have agreed on the following definition of the fuzzy restriction "low":

low = {1/1, .5/2, .1/3, .09/4, .001/5, 0/6}

Definitely numbers 4, 5, and 6 should not be considered as very low. This must be reflected in our definition of the hedge "very." The operator "very" must discriminate and decrease the fuzziness of "low" so that it disqualifies the numbers 4, 5, and 6 from "very low."

Earlier in this chapter, we saw that the operator CON will decrease the fuzziness of the elements of a fuzzy set in proportion to their degree of membership. The operator CON may provide a good definition for the hedge "very."

very low = CON (low)

CON(low)= {1/1, .25/2, .01/3, .0081/4, .000001/5, 0/6}

By combining the fuzzy operators that we have discussed so far, we can define a wide variety of hedges. The following are definitions of a few hedges. Remember that these definitions are subjective and you may define them differently.

```
(A) AND (B) = (FINTERS A B)

(A) OR (B) = (FUNION A B)

NOT (A) = (FCOMP A)

SORT OF (A) = (NORM (INT (DIL (A) AND INT (DEL (NOT
                                                     A))))

IN A SENSE (A) = (NORM (INT (A) AND NOT (A)))

SOMEWHAT (A) = (NORM (INT (DIL (A))))

ANYTHING BUT (A) = (NORM (INT (NOT A)))

VERY (A) = (CON A)

REASONABLY (A) = (CON (NORM (DIL (CON S)) AND (NORM
                                     (INT (CON A))))))

MORE OR LESS (A) = (NORM (INT (DIL (A)) AND (NOT
                                                A)))
```

Project 5.0

The idea in this programming project is to devise a program that uses the concepts of linguistic variables and the theory of fuzzy sets to perform natural language computation.

Assume that the universe is the set of positive integers from 1 to 6. Next, we define fuzzy restrictions to represent certain characteristics (for John), such as intelligent, handsome, and rich as follows:

```
(JOHN
        (intelligent
((1 0.2) (2 0.4) (3 1) (4 0.7) (5 0.3) (6 0.3)))
        (handsome
        ((1 0.1)(2 0.1) (3 0.3)(4 0.5)(5 1)(6 0.6)))
        (rich
        ((1 0.8) (2 0.5) (3 1) (4 0.8)(5 0.5)(6 0.8)))
    )
```

In the interpretation of these fuzzy restrictions remember that we are using the scale of 1 to 6 to describe these characteristics. For instance we are not saying that John is rich if he has 3 unit of money, but on the scale of 1 to 6 (in term of being rich) John is very close to 3.

Our program should then derive from this information the level of John's intelligence or tell us how handsome or rich is he.

```
>(fuzzy)
```

Who do you want more information about ?

```
>(do you know John ?)
```

What do you need to know about JOHN ?

```
>(would you say that he is an intelligent fellow?)
```

SORT OF INTELLIGENT

or

```
>(I heard that John is a rich man)
```

MORE OR LESS RICH

```
>(Is he handsome ?)
```

VERY HANDSOME

For the program to arrive at these results, we first must define our fuzzy restrictions for intelligence, handsomeness, and richness. These have been defined as follows:

```
(intelligent '((1 0.01)(2 0.1)(3 0.4)(4 0.6)(5
                                     0.8)(6 1.0)))
(rich '((1 0.01)(2 0.1)(3 0.4)(4 0.6)(5 0.8)(6
                                     1.0)))
(handsome '((1 0.01)(2 0.1)(3 0.4)(4 0.6)(5 0.8)(6
                                     1.0)))
```

To keep things simple, we are using the following hedges that have been defined earlier.

1) Sort of
2) In a sense
3) Somewhat
4) Anything but
5) Very
6) Not
7) Reasonably
8) More or less

The program must go through several steps before it can tell us that John is "sort of intelligent."

First, our program must find out what kind of characteristics we are looking for. Then it must apply our predefined hedges or fuzzy restrictions for intelligent.

```
(sort_of '((1 0.01)(2 0.1)(3 0.4)(4 0.6)(5 0.8)(6
                                     1.0)))
Outcome 1> ((1 0.02)(2 0.2)(3 0.73)(4 0.90)(5
                                     0.98)(6 1))

(in_a_sense '((1 0.01)(2 0.1)(3 0.4)(4 0.6)(5 0.8)(6
                                     1.0)))
Outcome 2> ((1 0.99)(2 0.9)(3 0.6)(4 0.68)(5 0.92)
                                     (6 1))

(somewhat '((1 0.01)(2 0.1)(3 0.4)(4 0.6)(5 0.8)(6
                                     1.0)))
Outcome 3> ((1 0.02)(2 0.2)(3 0.73)(4 0.90)(5
                                     0.98)(6 1))

(anything_but '((1 0.01)(2 0.1)(3 0.4)(4 0.6)(5
                                     0.8)(6 1.0)))
```

```
Outcome 4> ((1 1)(2 0.98) (3 0.68) (4 0.32) (5 0.08)
                                            (6 0))

(very '((1 0.01)(2 0.1)(3 0.4)(4 0.6)(5 0.8)(6
                                            1.0)))
Outcome 5> ((1 0.0) (2 0.01) (3 0.16) (4 0.36) (5
                                       0.64) (6 1))

(fnot '((1 0.01)(2 0.1)(3 0.4)(4 0.6)(5 0.8)(6
                                            1.0)))
Outcome 6> ((1 0.99) (2 0.9) (3 0.6) (4 0.4) (5 0.2)
                                            (6 0))

(reasonably '((1 0.01)(2 0.1)(3 0.4)(4 0.6)(5 0.8)(6
                                            1.0)))
Outcome 7> ((1 8e-016) (2 8e-008) (3 0.005243) (4
                                       0.134369)
(5 0.865631) (6 1))

(more_or_less '((1 0.01)(2 0.1)(3 0.4)(4 0.6)(5
                                       0.8)(6 1.0)))
Outcome 8> ((1 0.99) (2 0.9) (3 0.73) (4 0.90) (5
                                       0.98) (6 1))
```

Next, the program must find which of these outcomes matches best with John's intelligence (fuzzy restriction).

Many algorithms exist to perform the task of matching and translating to natural language expressions. One of the most straight-forward techniques is called Best Fit. Best Fit techniques work best when the set of possible natural language expressions is limited. Best Fit is achieved by calculating the Euclidean distance from given fuzzy sets (in our above example, John's intelligence) to each of the fuzzy sets representing each of the defined natural language expressions (above outcomes). The distance between two fuzzy sets A and B can be calculated as follows:

$$A = \{ da(i)/i \mid i \text{ is in } U\}$$

$$B = \{ db(i)/i \mid i \text{ is in } U\}$$

$$\text{distance } (A,B) = \sqrt{\left(\sum_{i=1}^{8} (da(i)-db(i))^2 \right)}$$

Next, the natural language expression that yields the shortest distance from A is the best fit for A and may be used as its natural language representation.

The following is the listing for the program FUZZY, along with its data base.

```
;
(AL
        (intelligent
          ((1  0.6)  (2  0.7)  (3  0.3)  (4  0.6)  (5  0.7)  (6
                                            0.7)))
        (handsome
          ((1  0.5)(2  0.6)  (3  0.4)(4  0.3)(5  0.1)(6
                                            0.3)))
        (rich
          ((1  0.9)  (2  0.8)  (3  0.7)  (4  0.4)(5  0.1)(6
                                            0.0)))
)
;
(JOHN
        (intelligent
          ((1  0.2)  (2  0.4)  (3  1)  (4  0.7)  (5  0.3)  (6
                                            0.3)))
        (handsome
          ((1  0.1)(2  0.1)  (3  0.3)(4  0.5)(5  1)(6  0.6)))
        (rich
          ((1  0.8)  (2  0.5)  (3  1)  (4  0.8)(5  0.5)(6
                                            0.8)))
)
;
(SAM
        (intelligent
          ((1  0.5)  (2  0.6)  (3  0.7)  (4  0.1)  (5  0.1)  (6
                                            0.1)))
        (handsome
          ((1  0.2)(2  0.3)  (3  0.5)(4  0.1)(5  0.1)(6
                                            0.0)))
        (rich
          ((1  0.5)  (2  0.8)  (3  0.7)  (4  0.2)(5  0.2)(6
                                            0.1)))
)
;
(PATRICK
        (intelligent
          ((1  0)  (2  0.1)  (3  0.4)  (4  0.5)  (5  0.8)  (6
                                            0.9)))
        (handsome
          ((1  0.2)(2  0.3)  (3  0.5)(4  0.6)(5  0.1)(6
                                            0.0)))
        (rich
          ((1  0.5)  (2  0.8)  (3  0.7)  (4  0.2)(5  0.2)(6
                                            0.1)))
```

```lisp
)
;
(SANDY
      (intelligent
        ((1 0.3) (2 0.5) (3 0.6) (4 0.8) (5 0.8)(6
                                                 0.9)))
      (handsome
        ((1 0.2)(2 0.3) (3 1.0)(4 0.9)(5 0.4)(6
                                               0.2)))
      (rich
        ((1 0.5) (2 1.0) (3 0.8) (4 0.2)(5 0.1)(6
                                                0.0)))
)
;
(SUE
      (intelligent
        ((1 0.3) (2 0.5) (5 4.6) (4 0.8) (5 0.8)(6
                                                 0.9)))
      (handsome
        (   (1 0.2)(2 0.3) (3 0.4)(4 0.7)(5 0.8)(6
                                                 0.9)))
      (rich
        ((1 0.9) (2 0.8) (3 0.7) (4 0.2)(5 0.1) (6
                                                 0.0)))
)
;
(SALLY
      (intelligent
        ((1 0.3) (2 0.5) (3 0.6) (4 0.8) (5 0.4)(6
                                                 0.3)))
      (handsome
        ((1 0.2)(2 0.3) (3 0.3)(4 0.9)(5 0.6)(6
                                              0.3)))
      (rich
        ((1 0.5) (2 0.8) (3 0.7) (4 0.2)(5 0.5) (6
                                                 0.2)))
)

;            FUZZY

(defun FUZZY ()
      (init)                   ;Initialize.
      (setq information        ;Open data base.
           (open-file "fuzzy.dat" ':input ))
      (read_data)              ;Read the data base.
      (close information)      ;Close the data base.
```

```lisp
        (describe (answer))      ;Have information?
)
;
(defun describe (s)
    (let ((m (car s))
       (s (cadr s)))
       (cond
            ((null s))           ;Nil.
            (T                   ;Find the linguistic
                                 ;variable.
                 (select nil (best_fit s (eval m))
                                            2)
                 (princ m)
                 (terpri))
       )
    )
)
;

;
;     open_file
; This function simply opens the file to read or
; write.

(defun open-file (fname read-write)
            (open fname :direction read-write)
)
;
;     read_data
; This function reads data from the data base.
;
(defun read_data ()
      (do ()
            ((null (associate_list (read information
                                        ))))

      )
)
;     associate_list
; Store physical characteristics in the name of a
; person.

(defun associate_list (item)
    (cond
       ((null item) nil)
```

```lisp
         (T                          ;Add a new name to the
                                     ;list.
              (add_names_to_list (car item))
              (set (car item)   ;Store it in the name.
                   (cdr item))
         )
    )
)
;
;       add_names_to_list

(defun add_names_to_list (name)
      (setq group (cons name group))
)
;
;       init
; Initialization.

(defun init ()
     (setq physical '(intelligent handsome rich)
             inf nil group '()
        intelligent '((1 0.01)(2 0.1)(3 0.4)(4 0.6)(5
                                       0.8)(6 1.0))
        rich '((1 0.01)(2 0.1)(3 0.4)(4 0.6)(5 0.8)(6
                                                1.0))
        handsome '((1 0.01)(2 0.1)(3 0.4)(4 0.6)(5
                                       0.8)(6 1.0)))
)
;
;       get_input
; Get input and call parser.

(defun get_input (msg list &optional name)
      (setq name (parse (response msg name) list))
)
;
;       parse
; This tail recursive procedure recognizes the name
; or physical characteristics in the input strings.
;
(defun parse (in list)
    (let ((token (car in)))
       (cond
              ((or (null token)  ;Boundary
                   (member token list)) ;In the list?
               token)          ;Return the found out.
```

```lisp
          (T                     ;Otherwise go deeper.
                (parse (cdr in) list))
        )
    )
)


;     answer
; This procedure uses association lists to respond
; to the user questions.

(defun answer ()
    (let
        (( name                 ;Get the name.
        (get_input "Who do you want more information
                                      about"
                group)))
        (cond
            ((null name)         ;Do not know the
                                 ;person?
                (sorry))
            (T                   ;Otherwise get physical.
                (setq phy
                (get_input "What do you need to
                            know about "
                physical name))
                (cond
                    ((null phy)  ;No information?
                        (sorry))
                    (T           ;Otherwise.
                        (assoc phy
                            (eval name)))
                )
            )
        )
    )
)
;     response
; Get the user response.

(defun response (msg &optional name)
        (terpri)                 ;New line
        (princ msg)              ;Ask the question.
        (if (not (null name))    ;print the name if
                                 ;any.
                (princ name)
        )
```

```lisp
        (princ " ?")
        (terpri)
        (read)                          ;Get response.
)
;       sorry

(defun sorry ()
        (terpri)
        (princ `(Sorry-- I cannot help you! ))
        (terpri)
)


;               sort_of
(defun sort_of (s)
(norm (funion (int (dil s)) (int (dil s)))))
)

;               in_a_sense
(defun in_a_sense (s) (norm (funion (int s) (fcomp
                                                s))))

;               defun somewhat
(defun somewhat (s) (norm (int (dil s))))
;

;               anything_but
(defun anything_but (s) (norm (int (fcomp s))))

;               very
(defun very (s) (con s))

;               fnot
(defun fnot (s) (fcomp s))

;               reasonably
(defun reasonably (s)
        (int (norm (finters (dil (con s)) (norm (int
                                        (con s)))))))
)

;               more_or_less
(defun more_or_less (s)
    (norm (funion (int (dil s)) (fcomp s)))
)
;               FUNION
```

```lisp
; This procedure takes two sets for its arguments
; and returns the fuzzy union of them.
(defun FUNION (s1 s2)
    (cond
        ((null s2) s1)          ;Boundary condition.
        ((assoc (caar s2) s1)   ;Is it member of both
                                ;sets?
            (funion
                (sub            ;Replace deg. of mem.
                                ;with max.
                    (max (car s2) (assoc (caar
                                         s2) s1))
                s1)
                (cdr s2)))
        (T                      ;Otherwise add it.
            (append (funion s1 (cdr s2)) (list
                                         (car s2))))
    )
)
;           max
(defun max (a1 a2)
    (let ((da1 (cadr a1))
          (da2 (cadr a2)))
        (cond
            ((> da1 da2) a1)  ;Return the bigger one.
            (T a2)
        )
    )
)
;           sub
(defun sub (item list)
(cond
        ((null list) '())       ;Boundary condition.
        ((equal (car item) (caar list)) ;Replace it.
            (cons item (cdr list)))
        (T    (cons (car list)  ;Go deeper.
                (sub item (cdr list)))))
    )
)
;           FINTERS
; This procedure takes two sets for its arguments
; and returns the fuzzy intersection of them.
(defun Finters (s1 s2)
    (cond
        ((null s2) nil)         ;Boundary condition.
```

```lisp
          ((assoc (caar s2) s1)    ;Is it member of both
                                   ;sets?
                   (cons                  ;Replace deg. of mem.
                                          ;with min.
                         (min (car s2) (assoc (caar s2) s1))
                         (finters s1 (cdr s2))))
          (T (finters s1 (cdr s2)))
      )

)

;          min
(defun min (a1 a2)
   (let ((da1 (cadr a1))
         (da2 (cadr a2)))
        (cond
            ((> da1 da2) a2)   ;Return the smaller.
            (T a1)
      )
   )
)
;          CON
;  This operator change the degree of each set
;  member to their square.
(defun CON (s)
    (let ((d (degree_of_first_element s)))
       (cond
            ((null s) '())     ;Boundary condition.
            (T (cons                 ; Square the degree.
                     (subst (square d) d (car s))
                     (con (cdr s))))
      )
   )
)
;          square
(defun square (n) (* n n) )

;
(defun degree_of_first_element (s)
   (cond
      ((null s) 0.0)
      (T (car (cdar s)))
      )
)
;          DIL
```

```lisp
; This operator calculates the dilation of fuzzy set
; by calculating the square root of the degree of
; membership of each element of the fuzzy set.
(defun DIL (s)
    (let ((d (degree_of_first_element s)))
      (cond
              ((null s) '())      ;Boundary.
              (T (cons            ;Get the square root of
                                  ;degree.
                  (subst (sqrt (float d)) d (car s))
                  (dil (cdr s)))))
      )
    )
)
;           INT
; The operator intensification, increases the degree
; of membership of an element that has a degree of
; membership greater than 0.5 and reduces the degree
; of membership of element whose degree of
; membership is less than 0.5.
(defun INT (s)
    (let ((d (degree_of_first_element s)))
                        ;Get degree of membership.
      (cond
              ((null s) '())      ;Boundary condition.
              ((and (<= d  0.5) (>= d 0))
                    (cons
                      (subst (* 2 (square d)) d
                                          (car s))
                      (int (cdr s))))
              (T   (cons          ;Otherwise decrease.
                      (subst (- 1 (* 2 (square (- 1
                                          d))))
                                d (car s))
                      (int (cdr s))))
      )
    )
)
;           NORM
; The operator normalization scale degree of all
; elements to the same base by dividing the degree
; of membership of all elements by the maximum
; degree.
(defun norm (s)
      (norm1 s (max_degree s 0))
)
```

```
;           max_degree
; Find out the maximum degree of membership in the
; fuzzy set.
(defun max_degree (s m)
   (cond
      ((null s) m)                 ;Boundary.
      ((< m (degree_of_first_element s)) ;Get the
                                      ;bigger one.
         (max_degree (cdr s)
                  (degree_of_first_element s)))
      (T    (max_degree (cdr s) m)); otherwise continue.
   )
)
;           norm1
(defun norm1 (s m)
   (let ((d (degree_of_first_element s)))
      (cond
            ((null s) '())      ;Boundary.
            (T (cons              ;Divide each degree by
                                ;max.
               (subst (/ d m) d (car s))
               (norm1 (cdr s) m)))
      )
   )
)
;           FCOMP
; This operator calculates the complement of fuzzy
; set by subtracting degree of membership from one.
(defun FCOMP (s)
   (let ((d (degree_of_first_element s)))
      (cond
            ((null s) '())      ;Boundary.
            (T (cons              ;subtract the degree
                                ;from one.
               (subst (- 1 d) d (car s))
               (fcomp (cdr s))))
      )
   )
)
;           distance
(defun distance (s1 s2)
   (do*
      ((i 1 (+ i 1))             ;Increment i.
      (sum 0 (+ sum (square   ;Calculate Euclidean
                                ;distance.
            (- (degree_of_first_element s1)
```

```
                     (degree_of_first_element s2)))))
         (s1 s1 (cdr s1))
         (s2 s2 (cdr s2)))
         ((= i 7) (sqrt sum))
      )
)
;              best_fit
; Find the closest linguistics variable.
(defun best_fit (s1 s2)
      (bf s1 s2 99999 )               ;Find out the closest
                                      ;operator.
)

;              bf
(defun bf (s1 s2 d)
      (do*
         ((i 1 (+ i 1))              ;Increment I.
          (tag 0)                    ;Reset tag.
          (s (select s2 i 1) (select s2 i 1))
          (dis (distance s1 s)  ;Get the distance.
             (distance s1 s)))
          ((= i 9) tag)             ;Return tag.
             (if (> d dis)
                  (setq d dis tag i))
      )
)

;              select
(defun select (s i t)
(cond
      ((= i 1)
            (if (= t 1)
                (sort_of s)
                (princ "SORT OF ")))
      ((= i 2)
            (if (= t 1)
                (in_a_sense s)
                (princ "IN A SENSE ")))
      ((= i 3)
            (if (= t 1)
                (somewhat s)
                (princ "SOMEWHAT ")))
      ((= i 4)
            (if (= t 1)
                (anything_but s)
                (princ "ANYTHING BUT ")))
```

```
((= i 5)
    (if (= t 1)
        (very s)
        (princ "VERY ")))
((= i 6)
    (if (= t 1)
        (fnot s)
        (princ "NOT ")))
((= i 7)
    (if (= t 1)
        (reasonably s)
        (princ "REASONABLY ")))
((= i 8)
    (if (= t 1)
        (more_or_less s)
        (princ "MORE OR LESS ")))
    )
)
```

The program FUZZY is a modification of programming project 3.0 with the addition of all the fuzzy operators that we have defined so far.

The procedure BEST_FIT carries out the Best Fit algorithm. The procedure SELECT has dual use. It either activates the appropriate hedge or returns the equivalent natural language expression.

References

For an excellent reading on fuzzy set see "Fuzzy Sets, Natural Language Computations, and Risk Analysis," by Kurt J. Schmucker.

The program in this chapter captures some of the definitions Zadeh proposes for various fuzzy set operations.

[1]. Zadeh A. L., "*Fuzzy Sets*", Information and Control, 1965.

[2]. Schmucker J. Kurt, "*Fuzzy Sets, Natural Language Computations, and Risk Analysis*", Computer Science Press, Rockville, MD, 1984.

[3]. Hoffman, L.J., Michelman, E. H. and Clements, D. "*SECURATE-Security Evaluation and Analysis Using Fuzzy Metrics*", Proceedings of the 1978 National Computer Conference, vol.47, AFIPS Press, Montvale, New Jersey, 1978.

[4]. Zadeh A. L., "*Quantitative Fuzzy Semantics*", Information Sciences, Vol. 3, no. 2, 1971.

[5]. Zadeh A. L., *"Fuzzy Languages and their Relation to Human and Machine Intelligence"*, Proceedings of the International Conference on Man and Computer, Karger, Bordeadux, 1970.

[6]. Zadeh A. L., *"Fuzzy Logic and Approximate Reasoning"*, Synthese, 1975.

[7]. Zadeh A. L., *"PURF- A Meaning Representation Language For Natural Language"*, International Journal Of Man-Machine, Studies 10, 1978.

[8]. Zadeh A. L. *"Fuzzy Sets versus Probability"*, Proceeding of IEEE, Vol. 68, no. 3, 1980.

[9]. Zadeh A. L., *"Common Sense Knowledge Representation Based on Fuzzy Logic"*, Computer, 1983.

[10]. Zadeh A. L., *"A Simple View of the Dempster- Shafer Theory of Evidence and Its Implication for the Rule of Combination"*, A.I. Magazine, 1986.

6

DESIGNING SYMBOLIC PATTERN MATCHING PROGRAMS

A system capable of matching symbolic expressions gives us a powerful tool, especially for designing and carrying out rule-based or expert systems. Because of the importance of symbolic pattern matching, it is one of the basic ingredients of many AI based software, this entire chapter deals with this topic.

This chapter begins with the basic ideas of symbolic pattern matching and proceeds by rewriting our chapter three programming project 3.1: VISION so that it employs a matching algorithm and separates rules (knowledge) from the program itself.

The chapter also explores the fuzzy matcher concept. Fuzzy matcher can be designed by integrating fuzzy set theory with the symbolic pattern matching system. The fuzzy matcher can be most useful in cases where the system neither succeeds nor fails but certain parts of one expression may match in some way with another expression. By employing linguistic variables, The fuzzy matcher, can describe the match as very low or "NOT AT ALL" to very high or "EXCELLENT."

Basic Ideas

The symbolic pattern matching system works by comparing one expression with another. The outcome is either a success, which means we have a match, or a failure in the case of no match. Let's call the first expression a pattern and the second one the base. Our simple procedure MATCH will give us the following results:

```
(match '(I have a little dog) '(I have a little
                                          dog))

>SUCCEED

(match '(I have a little dog) '(I have a little
                                          cat))

>FAIL
```

The syntax of our propose matcher is:

(MATCH Pattern Base)

Where pattern and base are lists.

```
;                   MATCH Ver. 1.0
; This program tries to find a match between two
; expressions, namely pattern and base.
(defun MATCH (p b)
    (cond
      ((and (null p) (null b)) 'succeed)  ;Succeed.
      ((or (null p) (null b)) 'fail)      ;Fail.
      ((equal (car p) (car b))            ;Continue
                                          ;the match.

          (match (cdr p) (cdr b)))
      (T 'FAIL)
      )
   )
```

Special Symbols

Special symbols such as wild card '*' and '?' can provide our matcher with a wider variety of patterns for performing the matching.

Symbol '?' can stand for any atom in a given pattern.

```
(match '(I have a little ?) '(I have a little dog))
```

```
> SUCCEED
```

Symbol '*' is like '?' but can match for more than one atom.

```
(match '(I have *) '(I have a little dog))
```

```
> SUCCEED
```

```
;                   MATCH  Ver. 2.0
(defun match (p b)
     (if (match1 p b)
          (print 'succeed)
          (print 'failed))
     (terpri)
   )
```

```
;                    match1
; This program tries to find a match between two
; expressions namely pattern and base. It accepts
; wild
; card symbols  such as '?', '*' in a pattern, that
; can represent one or more atom(s) respectively.
; The procedure is based on the chapter
; 17 "Symbolic Pattern Matching" of LISP by P. H.
; Winston and B. K. P. Horn
;
;
(defun MATCH1 (p b)
      (let
      ((carp (car p))
       (carb (car b))
       (cdrp (cdr p))
       (cdrb (cdr b)))
      (cond
            ((and (null p) (null b)) T)   ;Succeed.
            ((or (null p) (null b)) Nil) ;Fail.
            ((or (equ carp carb)
                (equ carp '?))
                            ;Does it contain '?'.
            (match1 cdrp cdrb))
            ((equ carp '*)
                            ;Is first element '*'.
            (or (match1 cdrp cdrb)
                            ;Advance both p and b.
                (match1 p cdrb)))
                            ;Advance only b.
      )
      )
)


;                    equ
(defun equ (a b)
      (cond
      ((and (numberp a)  (numberp b)
            (= a b)) T)
      ((and (symbolp a)  (symbolp b)
            (equal a b)) T)
      (T Nil)
      )
)
```

respectively. The procedure INFERENCE will be called next to start the cycle of matching, resolving conflict, and firing.

The procedure TRIGGER will trigger all the rules that satisfy the current situation of the facts in the data base. The predicate APPLICABLEP finds out whether the antecedent/consequent of a given rule can be satisfied by calling the procedure CLAUSE.

The global list BUFFER assigns a value to the pattern variable by using the procedure MATCH (Procedures MATCH, PULL_VALUE, PATTERN_VARIABLE are the same as before).

The procedure TRIGGER calls procedure RPT to replace the pattern variables of a rule with their values.

Two simple procedures, IFA and THENC, will simply return the IF part or THEN part of a rule, respectively.

Once the procedure INFERENCE contains the list of trigger rules, it will use the REMOVE_RULES procedure to remove all the rules that will not contribute anything new to the data base.

Procedure FIRE takes the list of triggered rules as its argument. It calls SELECT_RULE to resolve the conflict and then fires the selected rule. Procedure SELECT_RULE is an implementation of a size-ordering algorithm for resolving a conflict among the triggered rules. It will select a rule with the longest list of antecedents and in the case of a tie, will select the first rule.

Once a rule has been fired, our data base must be updated. This is the function of the procedure RECORD, which will record only the clauses that are not in the data base.

The procedure EXPLAIN explains the reasoning of each iteration. It can explain how or why it has deduced new facts, by listing the triggered rules, the fired rule, and the consequences thereby deduced.

Backward_Chaining

Backward_chaining will move from the goal state (hypothesis) backwards toward the initial states (premises). It works the same as forward_chaining but, instead of matching the assertions in the data base with the antecedent, backward_chaining matches goals against the consequent. In case of a match, it will trigger the rule. It uses conflict resolution to select a rule to fire. Once a rule has fired, the data base will be updated.

Backward_chaining works best when the shape of the state space is "fan out." Fan out situations occur when a problem contains a limited number of initial states and many goal states. See fig. 7.1.

Backward-chaining Algorithm:

I. Repeat until either the initial state is reached or no consequent of any rule can match a goal.

    I.1. Trigger all the rules whose consequent(s) can be satisfied by the goals.

    I.2. If more than one rule has been triggered, apply conflict resolution mechanism to choose one rule for firing.

    I.3. If the antecedent(s) of the fired rule can be satisfied by the symbols in the data base, then add its consequent(s) to the data-base. Otherwise make the antecedent of the fired rule a new subgoal and add it to the goal list.

If we apply backward-chaining inference program to the "RULES0.BAS" we will have:

```
(BACKWARD_CHAIN)

> Please enter the name of the knowledge base : >
  "rules0.bas"

Please enter facts, separate each fact by enclosing
it in the parenthesis.
> ((A) (C))

Please enter goals:> ((F))

Working on goal ((F))

These rules have been triggered: (RULE5)

From trigger rules-  RULE5 has been fired.
In order to show (F) is true,
we have to establish a new subgoal, ((D))
and show that it is true.

Working on goal ((D) (F))

These rules have been triggered: (RULE3 RULE5)

From trigger rules-  RULE3 has been fired.
I already know that ((A) (C)) is true
```

```
Therefore; (D) must be true too.
Data base now contains the following symbols:
((A) (C) (D))

Working on goal ((F))

These rules have been triggered: (RULE5)

From trigger rules-  RULE5 has been fired.
I already know that ((D)) is true
Therefore; (F) must be true too.
Data base now contains the following symbols:
((A) (C) (D) (F))

No more rules can be triggered.
```

Just as in FORWARD_CHAINING, we have to supply the system with the name of the rule base and list of facts in the data base (premises). Our program BACKWARD_CHAINING also requires the list of goals or hypotheses that must be proved. In this example, we assume A and C are known to be true and we want to prove F is true, too. Our BACKWARD_CHAIN first starts with the goal (F) and looks at the rules which might yield that conclusion. Rule 5 matches our criteria, since:

D -> F

Therefore rule 5 is fired, which will result in adding a new goal (D) to our goal list. Now (D) becomes our new subgoal and we have to prove that it is true. Our program chains on as before and selects rule 3 since its consequent matches our new subgoal. Rule 3 is defined as follows:

A & C -> D

Since we know (A) and (C) are true (they are given facts in our data base), therefore (D) must be true too. (D) is a fact now and can be added to our data base, and since (D) is true, (F) is true also. This is exactly what our backward chaining program has done.

The following data base contains pattern variables, as follows:

```
(Rule rule1
    (IF
            ((< man1) is the father of (< man2))
            ((< man1) is the father of (< man3)))
    (THEN
            ((> man2) and (> man3) are brothers)
            ((< man2) is a son of (> man1))
            ((< man3) is a son of (> man1)))
)
```

```
(Rule rule2
      (IF
            ((< man1) is a male)
            ((< man2) is a son of (< man1)))
      (THEN
            ((> man1) is the father of (> man2)))
)

(Rule rule3
      (IF
            ((< man1) is the father of (< man2))
            ((< man2) is the father of (< man3)))
      (THEN
            ((> man1) is the grandfather of (> man3))
            ((> man2) is a son of (< man1))
            ((< man3) is a son of (< man2)))
)

(Rule rule4
      (IF
            ((< man1) is the father of (< man2))
            ((< man3) is the father of (< man1)))
      (THEN
            ((> man3) is the grandfather of (> man2))
            ((> man1) is a son of (< man3))
            ((< man2) is a son of (< man1)))
)

(Rule rule5
      (IF
            ((< man1) and (< man2) are brothers)
            ((< man2) is the father of (< man)))
      (THEN
            ((> man1) is the uncle of (> man))
            ((> man2) is a male))
)

(Rule rule6
      (IF
            ((< man) is the father of (< child)))
      (THEN
            ((> child) is a child of (> man)))
)


(BACKWARD_CHAIN)
```

228

```
; loading "bchain.lsp"
> Please enter the name of the knowledge base : >
"rules2.bas"

Please enter facts, separate each fact by enclosing
it in the parenthesis.
>((tom is a male)(jack is a son of tom))

Please enter goals:> ((jack is a child of tom))

Working on goal ((JACK IS A CHILD OF TOM))

These rules have been triggered: (RULE6)

From trigger rules- RULE6 has been fired.
In order to show (JACK IS A CHILD OF TOM) is true,
we have to establish a new subgoal, ((TOM IS THE
FATHER OF JACK))
and show that it is true.

Working on goal ((TOM IS THE FATHER OF JACK) (JACK
IS A CHILD OF TOM))

These rules have been triggered: (RULE2 RULE6)

From trigger rules- RULE2 has been fired.
I already know that ((TOM IS A MALE) (JACK IS A SON
OF TOM)) is true
Therefore; (TOM IS THE FATHER OF JACK) must be true
too.
Data base now contains the following symbols:
((TOM IS A MALE) (JACK IS A SON OF TOM) (TOM IS THE
FATHER OF JACK))

Working on goal ((JACK IS A CHILD OF TOM))

These rules have been triggered: (RULE6)

From trigger rules- RULE6 has been fired.
I already know that ((TOM IS THE FATHER OF JACK)) is
true
Therefore; (JACK IS A CHILD OF TOM) must be true
too.
Data base now contains the following symbols:
((TOM IS A MALE) (JACK IS A SON OF TOM) (TOM IS THE
FATHER OF JACK)
(JACK IS A CHILD OF TOM))

No more rules can be trigger.
```

Again our program BACKWARD_CHAIN is started from hypotheses ((tom is a male) (jack is a son of tom)) backward to prove (jack is a child of tom).

The following is the listing for the program BACKWARD_CHAIN. ;

```
              BACKWARD CHAINING INFERENCE PROGRAM
(defun BACKWARD_CHAIN ()      ;Backward_chain
                              ;inference.
       (read_rules            ;Read rules.
           (open_file (fn) ':input))
       (get_input)            ;Get the facts and
                              ;goals
       (inference)            ;Inference.
       (terpri)
)
;                   backward_chain
(defun inference ()
     (do*
          ((tr (trigger rule '()) ;Trigger rules.
               (trigger rule '()))
           (r (remove_rules tr)     ;Remove repetition.
              (remove_rules tr))
           (fr (fire r) (fire r)) ;Fire the rule.
           (antecedent (ifa fr) (ifa fr)))
                    ;Antecedent of fired rule.
          ((or (null goals) (null fr)) ;No rules can
                                       ;be fired.
            (princ "\nNo more rules can be
                             triggered."))
           (explain_rules tr fr goals)
           (cond
                ((applicablep antecedent data-
                     base) ;Is antecedent true?
                 (record_symbols
                      (list (car goals)))
                      ;add it to data-base.
                 (explain_new_symbol
                      antecedent (car goals))
                 (setq goals (cdr goals)))
                 ;Remove it from the goal.
                (T

                 (explain_new_goal antecedent)
                 (record_goals antecedent))
                     ;Establish a new goal.

          )
```

```lisp
        )
)
;                open_file
(defun open_file (fname read-write)
     (open fname :direction read-write)
)
;                read_rules
(defun read_rules (data)
     (setq rule '())
     (do ()
          ((null (associate_list (read data)))))
     )
)
;                associate_list
(defun associate_list (item)
     (cond
          ((null item) nil)
          (T (setq rule (append rule (list item))))) 
     )
)


;          add_list
; Add new item to Associate list.
(defun add_list (lst item )
     (append lst (list item))
)
;                fn
(defun fn ()
   (princ "Please enter the name of the knowledge
                                        base : ")
   (read)
)
;                get_input
;Get the facts and the goals
(defun get_input ()
   (princ "\n\n\n\nPlease enter facts, separate ")
   (princ "each fact by enclosing it \n")
   (princ "in the parenthesis.\n")
   (setq data-base (read))
   (princ "\nPlease enter goals:")
   (setq goals (read))
)
;                explain_rules
; Report the trigger rules and fired rule.
(defun explain_rules (tr fr g)
   (princ "\nWorking on goal ")
```

```lisp
    (print g)
    (princ "\nThese rules have been triggered: ")
    (print (rules tr))
    (princ "\nFrom trigger rules-  ")
    (princ (car (rules (list fr))))
    (princ " has been fired.\n")
)
;                    explain_new_symbol
; Report the new deduce facts
(defun explain_new_symbol (ante conse)
    (princ "I already know that ")
    (princ ante)
    (princ " is true\n")
    (princ "Therefore; ")
    (princ  conse)
    (princ " must be true too.\n")
    (princ "Data base now contains the following
    symbols:\n")
    (print  data-base)
)
;                    explain_new_goals
;Report the new goal
(defun explain_new_goal (ante)
    (princ "In order to show ")
    (princ (car goals))
    (princ " is true,\n")
    (princ "we have to establish a new subgoal, ")
    (princ ante)
    (princ " and show that it is true.\n")
)


;                    rules
(defun rules (r)
    (cond
            ((null r) '())              ;Boundary
            (T (cons (cadr (car r))
                                ;Return the rule ID.
                (rules (cdr r)))))
    )
)
;                    record_goals
; add a new consequent to list of goals, this will
; become our new subgoal.
(defun record_goals (symbol)
    (cond
```

```lisp
            ((null symbol))
            ((or (applicablep (list (car symbol))
                                      goals)
                 (applicablep (list (car symbol))
                                      data-base))
                    (record_goals (cdr symbol)))
            (T (setq goals         ;Add the new goal.
                 (append (list (car symbol)) goals))
                 (record_goals (cdr symbol))))
      )
)
;                    record_symbol
; add the new symbols to the data base

(defun record_symbols (symbol)
    (cond
            ((null symbol))
            ((applicablep (list (car symbol))
                                   data-base)
                    (record_symbols(cdr symbol)))
        (T (setq data-base        ;Add the new goal.
                 (append  data-base (list
                                        (car symbol)))))
                 (record_symbols(cdr symbol)))
      )
)
;                        remove
;Remove duplications.
(defun remove_rules (r)
    (cond
            ((null r) '())
            ((applicablep (ifa (car r)) goals)
                 (remove_rules (cdr r)))
            (T (cons (car r) (remove_rules (cdr r)))))
      )
)
;                      applicablep
;This predicate takes two lists and then checks to
;see that all the elements of the first list match
;the second list.

(defun applicablep (ante-conse data)
    (cond
            ((null ante-conse) T)   ;Rule is
                                    ;applicable.
```

```
                    (T (let ((d (clause (car ante-conse)
                                        data)))
                    (cond
            ((null d) nil)   ;Not applicable.
                    (T (applicablep (cdr ante-conse)
                                    (remove d data)))
                    )
                )
            )
        )
    )
;                       clause
;Clause calls match to see if two clauses match.
(defun clause (item lst)
    (cond
            ((null lst) nil)
            ((match item (car lst) buffer) (car lst))
            (T (clause item (cdr lst)))
        )
    )

;                       trigger
;
; Trigger all the rules whose consequents match the
; data base or goals.
(defun trigger (lst rules)
    (let ((r (car lst)))
        (setq buffer '())
        (cond
            ((null lst) rules)         ;Returns the
                                       ;triggered rules.
            ((applicablep (thenc r) goals)
                        ;Add it to the trigger rules.
                    (trigger (cdr lst)
                        (append rules (list (rpi
                                            r)))))
            (T  (trigger (cdr lst) rules))
        )
    )
)

;                       fire
;Fire a rule by resolving the conflict, if any.
(defun fire (rules)
    (cond
            ((null rules) nil)       ;Nil.
```

Wong, G. W., *"PC Scheme: A Lexical LISP"*, Byte, Vol. 12, No. 3, 1987, 223-5.

Wong, G. W., *"BYSO LISP AND WALTZ LISP"*, Byte, Vol. 11, No. 7, 1986, 293-6.

Wong, G. W., *"Arity/Prolog"*, Byte, Vol. 11, No. 3, 1986, 245-8.

Wong, G. W., *"TLC-LISP"*, Byte, Vol. 10, No. 10, 1985, 287-292.

Woods, B. T., *"What's in a Link: Foundations for semantic Networks"*, In D. G. Bobrow and A. Collins, eds., Representation and Understanding: Studies in Cognitive Science, Academic Press, New York, NY, 1975.

Zadeh A. L., *"Fuzzy Sets"* ,Information and Control, 1965.

Zadeh A. L., *"Quantitative Fuzzy Semantics"*, Information Sciences, Vol. 3, no. 2, 1971.

Zadeh A. L., *"Fuzzy Languages and their Relation to Human and Machine Intelligence"*, Proceedings of the International Conference on Man and Computer, Karger, Bordeadux, 1970.

Zadeh A. L., *"Fuzzy Logic and Approximate Reasoning"*, Synthese, 1975.

Zadeh A. L., "PURF- A Meaning Representation Language For Natural Language", International Journal Of Man-Machine, Studies 10, 1978.

Zadeh A. L. *"Fuzzy Sets versus Probability"*, Proceeding of IEEE, Vol. 68, no. 3, 1980.

Zadeh A. L., *"Common Sense Knowledge Representation Based on Fuzzy Logic"*, Computer, 1983.

Zadeh A. L., *"A Simple View of the Dempster-Shafer Theory of Evidence and Its Implication for the Rule of Combination"*, A.I. Magazine, 1986.

INDEX

An Invitation

Sigma Press is still expanding—and not just in computing, for which we are best known. Our marketing is handled by John Wiley and Sons Ltd, the UK subsidiary of a major American publisher. With our speed of publication and Wiley's marketing skills, we can make a great success of your book on both sides of the Atlantic.

Currently, we are looking for new authors to help us to expand into many exciting areas, including:

Laboratory Automation
Communications
Electronics
Professional Computing
New Technology
Personal computing
Artificial Intelligence
General Science
Engineering Applications

If you have a practical turn of mind, combined with a flair for writing, why not put your talents to good use? For further information on how to make a success of your book, write to:

Graham Beech, Editor-in-Chief, Sigma Press,
98a Water Lane, Wilmslow, Cheshire SK9 5BB
or, phone 0625-531035